The Ground Aslant

The Ground Aslant

—An Anthology of Radical Landscape Poetry—

edited by

Harriet Tarlo

Shearsman Books
Exeter

First published in the United Kingdom in 2011 by
Shearsman Books Ltd
58 Velwell Road,
Exeter EX4 4LD

ISBN 978-1-84861-081-1
First Edition

Editor's Acknowledgements
Many thanks to Julia Ball and Frances Presley for longstanding inspiration;
Tony Frazer for his belief in the project and long hours of labour; the contributors for their work
and their patience, and Simon, Laura and Ben for support knowing and unknowing.

Contents

Introduction

anthologising

This anthology is testament to the originality and dynamism of recent landscape poetry, poetry which engages with place, locality and "nature" (or what we have left of it). It is not of course that there has been no previous landscape writing within the modernist tradition. Many of these poets look back to Basil Bunting and to Ian Hamilton Finlay, for instance, and across the water too to poets such as Lorine Niedecker and Charles Olson. Yet, there does seem to be a growing momentum to landscape writing and this perhaps reflects the growing political and ecological importance of our relationship to our environment. In this work, the relationship between human beings, their fellow-creatures and the land we live in is under close and scrupulous examination. The subtitle of *The Ground Aslant,* makes use of a term I have worked with for a decade or more, "radical landscape poetry". The word "landscape" is a compound, of the land itself and the "scape" which acknowledges interventionist human engagement with land. In common parlance, this may be literal landscaping by gardeners or designers or it may be the representation of land in art. The landscaping between these covers is not unrelated: it takes a view or perspective on land, linguistically or philosophically shaping the specific or generic land with which it engages.

Landscape is wide and broad; even "radical landscape" is still fairly open. It does not dictate, circumscribe or limit the work over-much, either in terms of form or politics, but it does assume a degree of radicalism. This is appropriate, not least because landscape poetry often challenges the divide between experimental or innovative and traditional or mainstream which has haunted British poetry, in all its many guises, since the nineteen-thirties. The challenge emerges from the fact that, however innovative, this work attempts to be, to cite Charles Olson, "Equal, That Is, to the Real Itself". It clings to its hold on the local and physical world; it is "from here", to quote from Skoulding's sequence from which our title comes. "The Ground Aslant" also evokes Emily Dickinson, one of the early innovators of "telling it slant". Finally, it touches on Peter Larkin's use of the word "aslant" throughout the vertiginously titled 'Lean Earth Off Trees Unaslant', a long poem considering human perspective, returning us again to that taking of a view, to our human "scaping" of the land in art.

It is perhaps surprising, on such a small island, that I should have found it hard to narrow down my selection of innovative landscape poetry to sixteen poets. Tony Frazer, editor of Shearsman Books, made the point early on that we should try to include a reasonable number of pages for each poet. The longer I worked on the anthology, the more I came to agree with this view. I wanted the reader to be able to gain a sense of the richness of the work of the poets included. I felt this even more strongly because many of the most exhilarating landscape poems in recent years have been long poems or sequences which prove difficult to represent. The only complete sequence included here is Thomas A. Clark's 'The Grey Fold'. Clark's poetry is largely sequential, working through incremental small changes in language and perception, page by page. It is therefore fitting to represent him with one work in this way. With other poets, such as

Colin Simms, Peter Riley, Peter Larkin, Wendy Mulford and Zoë Skoulding, I have attempted to select from long works in order to give a feel of those texts and, I hope, to send readers out to seek the originals. For those interested in the landscape sequence or long poem, I would suggest returning to the landmark English modernist poem of landscape, Bunting's *Briggflatts*. More recently, the sequences of two poets who certainly would have been represented here if they had still been with us, Richard Caddel's 'Ground' and Barry MacSweeney's 'Pearl', are very much worth reading.

All the writers included in this anthology are contemporary poets whose contribution to the field is significant. Many poets engage with place and environment in some way or some work, but landscape writing is central to the practice of the poets published here. I do feel some sense of redressing a balance here. There were several decades when the urban was seen as providing more appropriate material for the experimental poet and one still sees hints of that feeling even in the poets themselves. "As I re-read these poems there may be too much landscape", writes Ian Davidson in the afterword to his book, *At a Stretch*. He goes on to justify this with descriptions of his work which are relevant to much of what is published here, for instance the inter-relationship between the local and the global and "how speech and writing might jump from place to place and terminal to terminal" (109). Yet, it is interesting that such justification is felt necessary, that the relevance of landscape writing still has to be argued.

In terms of organisation, poets are presented in chronological order, enabling the reader to trace the development of radical landscape poetries and to see connections and diversifications emerge through time. The work of some younger poets has been encouraged and promoted by older writers here. Readers might like, for instance, to consider Nicholas Johnson as an inheritor of Barry MacSweeney's poetry, Helen Macdonald of Peter Riley's and Mark Dickinson of Peter Larkin's. I have also presented the work of each poet in order of previous publication, with unpublished work appearing at the end of each poet's segment of the book. I wanted, as far as possible within the limitations of space, to convey a sense of each writer's *oeuvre*.

form

I have focused here on poets whose formal techniques are exploratory and experimental enough to be called radical, poets whose ideological pushing of the boundaries is to be found integrated into the forms their poems inhabit. I chose work, in part, to represent the diversity of these forms. Difference is often located in the use of space on the page. In the early Tony Baker, in Elisabeth Bletsoe and in my own work, we see the classic fluid use of open form text. But a closer look soon demonstrates the diversity that open form can take, from Colin Simms' dynamic shift from left to right in 'Snowy Owl' and 'Otter Dead in Water' to Wendy Mulford's and Frances Presley's use of central justification in *The East Anglia Sequence* and 'Alphabet for Alina', to Mark Dickinson's use of the grid in 'The Speed of Clouds'. Looking deeper into one writer's work shows the care open-form poets bring to the page, as a reading of Presley's thirty-five stone setting and longstone poems shows. Even the four included here demonstrate how each piece is shaped and written in a way which relates to the individual stones and their landscapes.[1] Clearly, there is a relationship between the spatial arrangement of the poem and the landscape, a sense that we feel all around us when entering the dense columns of Larkin's 'Slights Agreeing Trees' and Skoulding's 'Through Trees', or when tracing the fragmented, floating words in Dickinson's poems from 'The Speed of Clouds'.

Several poems, such as Mulford's 'East Anglia Sequence', Larkin's 'Open Woods', my own Workington poems and Bletsoe's 'Cross in Hand' juxtapose differing arrangements of prose blocks, found text and stanzas of poetry, each within their own spaces. These diverse texts speak to each other across the space, allowing readers to enter the poem and speculate over their relationship to each other. We find a similar opportunity to be a creative (or, in Roland Barthes' sense of the word, "writerly") reader in the telling, breathing spaces between phrases in Carol Watts' and Mark Goodwin's poems and the widely separated lines at the end of Mark Dickinson's *Littoral xxi*. All these forms affect the reading, the sounding of the poem in the air, and this is central to the philosophy of the open form poem. The use of space on the page and sound off the page are two of the most important ways in which landscape is explored in this work. This is felt as powerfully as anywhere in Thomas A Clark's short poems existing in wide, deep space on the page. Here the relationship between form and space (place) is symbiotic, just as Clark finds "space for a form" in the play of moss and fern in 'The Grey Fold'.

As we move from considering the spatial to the sonic, the work which inhabits the page more conventionally comes into focus. Any delving into British or American avant-garde poetry soon teaches us that a continuous text does not make for continuity of narrative or discourse. In the poetry of Peter Riley, Ian Davidson and Helen Macdonald, it is the language itself that dances and defies expectation. Seemingly deceptively simple, Riley in particular opens up mental spaces we don't expect. It is in the sonic chiming and spatial proximity of "business" and "bitterness" in Riley's 'Shining Cliff' poem that a wealth of meanings lie, just as they do between the proximity of "politics" and "polite" in Davidson's 'Human Remains and Sudden Movements'. Throughout all these poetries, juxtaposition (often through parataxis) is a fundamental linguistic principle. Here we find different discourses of nature or place, whether it be the use of natural and unnatural terminologies in Skoulding or the meeting of scientific and spiritual language in Dickinson. Similarly, landscape words appear and are interrogated throughout, the "submerged etymologies of such words as 'garden', 'enclosure', 'boundary wall'" (Bletsoe) reverberating through the poems. Perhaps the most paratactic linguistic display is in the funny-profound, fast-moving phrases of Tony Baker's journey through life's places and spaces, 'Quilt', its first stanza leaping from joke-opening to the provokingly unfinished, mulled-over line, "the land escapes because it refuses". Here, once again, the play is linguistic not spatial, as readers leap over boundaries between discourses to construct new meanings for themselves.

Language is a form in which landscape can come alive. Colin Simms inherits through his great mentor, Basil Bunting, the use of alliterative and compound words, forms of kenning which Bunting regarded as derived from a Northern tradition associated with Old Norse and the Gawain poet. Poetry and landscape are images for each other in these lines from *Briggflatts*: "Rime is crisp on the bent,/ ruts stone-hard, frost spangles fleece".[2] In Bunting and in Simms words are frequently yoked together to convey a sensation which they could not achieve alone, and to invoke and enact energy. This particularly evident in 'Loch Maree 1970' where the fluid movement of the otter is enacted through compound words and flowing lines free of punctuation. Nicholas Johnson and Mark Goodwin use similar linguistic techniques. In Johnson's poetry, influenced perhaps by MacSweeney's kenning, we find a sound-based lyricism flowing through pieces such as 'Haul Song'. In Goodwin's more recent work, such as 'Passing Through Sea-Thorn', words begin to split and splinter into their linguistic components or energy compounds.

Ultimately all these poets recognise in their own ways that, particularly when engaging with landscape, "language can only take you so far" (Davidson). In Mulford's one letter lines and Johnson's 'Eel Earth' the form and sound of each individual phoneme becomes powerful in its own terms. We feel the landscape that is beyond language; so all the complex thought about life, land and politics in Presley's 'North Hill' fades out with the sea, not described or discussed, but sounded:

> sur sur sur sur
> sur surring
>
> su su   su   rus

terminologies

As I hinted above, several of the contributors to this book write with an additional edge and urgency in the face of the environmental crisis. Peter Larkin acknowledges that one of his concerns is "with matters of landscape and ecology, often focussing on the predicament and analogical patterning of the woods and plantations which residually border our lives".[3] Before it became common knowledge, Simms, a naturalist as well as a poet, was warning his readers of the threat. 'The Crags at Crookleth Beacon' begins with a charmed Wordsworthian picture of the child in nature, but soon turns to humanity's destructive impulse with the words, "an hour destroys the kestrels' home". Similarly uncompromising are Wendy Mulford references to coastal erosion in 'The East Anglia Sequence', Frances Presley's to global warming in 'Triscombe stone' and Tony Baker's "soils/ worn thin for nitrogen . . ." ('aurals xiv').

I have argued elsewhere that it is possible that poetry within the experimental tradition could be particularly powerful in its contribution to the necessary mental and emotional adjustments to environment that we need, urgently, to make.[4] However, this is not a book of polemical ecopoetry or even of ecopoetics, the more innovative tendency espoused in the journal of the same name.[5] Rather, this is a book of radical landscape poetry, some of which may also be motivated by environmentalism. Although some landscape poets may be ecopoets and some ecopoets may be landscape poets, the two are by no means interchangeable. Equally individual poems may be one and not the other. I decided against including in this anthology one of my favourite poems by Tony Baker, 'You Tell Me', because I could not describe it as a landscape poem. In this piece, the natural elements come to the poet rather than the poet going out into the natural world. In this poem, and in ecopoetic work in general, the poet ventures beyond landscape into a wider political and global sphere, just as in landscape poetry the poet's territory can be narrower or broader than the ecopolitical. Indeed some of the writers here, such as Mark Dickinson, are uncomfortable with the eco-poetry label, perhaps because of the emphasis on subject matter over form.

There is another, much older, sub-genre that landscape poetry is sometimes classified within, and often engages self-consciously with, and that is pastoral. As his preface to *Alstonefield*, Peter Riley publishes extracts from two letters to Tony Baker. Here he writes, partly though not entirely self-mockingly: "to work the selfhood through the fairground of its respite, and throw a shadow of truth or at least a critique, back to the rest of the known (Now that *is* a theory of pastoral!)" (7). Often there is an element of critique or parody in the poetry itself. In Ian Davidson's 'Human Remains and Sudden Movements', we find reference to "what England expects/ Fields full of Daffodils", lines which gain greater ironic edge by the use of capitals and the Welsh context for this piece. In 'C' from 'Alphabet for Alina', Frances Presley seems haunted by bygone pastoral images of harvest even as the modern stubbly John Barleycorn emerges. The poem cuts off at a moment of pathos, or perhaps bathos.

Whereas Pastoral often sentimentalises the rural life, radical landscape poetry is more realistic in its view of contemporary landscape, rural people and past and present agricultural and social issues. Indeed, the rural working class poet and great resister of enclosure, John Clare, is a significant ancestor to several of these poets. The harsh realities of rural life past and present were powerfully evoked in Barry MacSweeney's long poem, *Pearl*. Nicholas Johnson, a publisher and advocate of MacSweeney, does the same in 'West Chapple', published here, and in his longer autobiographical works, *Pelt* and *Show*. Carol Watts' poems from the emerging sequence 'Zeta Landscape' are a radical experiment in writing what she describes as "lyric nature poetry put under pressure". She confronts a specific farming environment through calculus and economics, creating a harmonic pattern of poems, each named after a prime number and each having nineteen lines. Through this process, she opens up the world of small scale farming, '7' in particular questioning our notions of value in relation to animal stock. Her internal mathematical logic also works outwards into the topography of a particular place, Rhosybreidden, a hill farm on the banks of the Vyrnwy river.[6] While Watts refuses to romanticise farming, at a linguistic and sonic level, the work is easily as beautiful and full of feeling as a piece of pastoral, a word she herself uses somewhat ironically in the first poem of the sequence. Here, in a fine old modernist tradition, we find ample examples of work which resists narrative and realist *conventions* in poetry in favour of evolving techniques and structures which aim to create a truer reflection of reality itself.

Ultimately, this contemporary poetry contemplates a world that has moved so far away from the landscapes out of which pastoral was born, that it can no longer be seen to be within the pastoral in an unproblematic way. At the heart of pastoral lies the morally and socially-inflected contrast between the cultural/urban and the natural which has, century by century, decade by decade, become increasingly outdated, especially in a small, crowded island like our own. We can no longer indulge in the simple pleasures of the "retreat and return" approach to nature. In general, if one can generalise about sixteen poets' work, this poetry does attempt to resist the sentimental attachment to landscape, even as it often acknowledges this as both legacy and temptation. Greg Garrard notes, "At the root of pastoral is the idea of nature as a stable enduring counterpoint to the disruptive energy and change of human societies".[7] This pastoral view of a "stable and harmonious nature" was not only present in literature, but in early ecology, and lingers in both fields today (57). More recent ecological thinking now understands that nature, although it strives for equilibrium, does so through a process characterised more by change than stasis and this contributes to the shift away from any "supposedly authentic or pristine state of nature" (58). This radical landscape poetry works in ways close to this thinking, the poems themselves embodying this sense of constant change. This is a poetry full of questions, uncertainties, self doubts and self-correction.

There is a recognition that this process of shift and adaptation occurs in a world in which natural and cultural, wild and urban or industrial elements exist in all those places where we exist. Peter Larkin's *Slights Agreeing Trees* explores the interplay between them in a teasing game of compare and contrast between pylon and tree. In the fragment from Peter Riley's 'Shining Cliff' we see and hear the A6 from the Derbyshire peaks. Zoë Skoulding's 'From Here' explores the landscape in and of the city, often employing urban language about the city and "natural" language about the urban. In Tony Baker's untitled poem beginning "storm clouds" small details evoke the village life of Birchover within the context of the bird-life above the Derbyshire White Peak village. This short unpretentious poem does not claim to contain the place it evokes: "It *won't* cohere", says Baker of a flock of pigeons, but surely also of his own human perception. Similarly, the clouds gather "with that persistent/ impulse belongs to other matter". These words seem echoed in Ian Davidson's lines from 'Human Remains and Sudden Movements': "I wrote specifically as if I could do otherwise/ The totality escapes me the folds that matter makes up".

Ultimately I feel that the self-reflective and critical nature of this work prevents it from being easily subsumed within the various manifestations of pastoral and ecopoetics. Its territory lies somewhere betwixt and between.[8]

the Scape

In diverse ways, all the poetry presented here remains concerned with the connections between the poet and the landscape, an age-old poetic relationship often associated with the Romantic age. Here it is again, but this time explored in the context, not only of that history, but also of all the variety, intimacy, complicity and complexity of modernity. Here there is never an easy assumption of the poet's knowledge or power. Close observation, but not over-assumption, is at the heart of this writing: "never mind the economics of the trip/ give me a poetry of observed relationship", to cite Simms' characteristically ironic summative couplet from 'The Crags at Crookleth Beacon'. Intimate observation of and involvement with a particular place remains at the heart of much landscape poetry, radical or otherwise. This is located writing. Very often, as with Simms, Mulford and Presley, the time and place of the piece is part of the poem. Most commonly, these poets have worked with places they live in or know well: Thomas A Clark with the Scottish Highlands, Presley with Minehead and Exmoor, Davidson with Anglesey and I myself with the Holme Valley. Yet these poets also move out from the local to engage with places further afield. Johnson's *Cleave* begins at home in the Devonshire countryside beset by the horrors of Foot and Mouth. But in the final poem, 'The Stars have broken in pieces' the poet journeys through the "debatable lands" of England in an elegiac poem scattered with a litany of English place names. Further afield yet, Simms and Riley have written American sequences, two of which (Simm's 'Carcajou: A Poem of Encounter' and Riley's 'Western States') are extracted here.

The most fruitful relationship with place seems often to involve a degree of intimacy and of distance. Peter Riley lived near Alstonefield in North Staffordshire for four years, but it was his return as a visitor that prompted him to begin writing his sequence of place, *Alstonefield*. In the preface he writes to Baker, "everyday sights do diminish so, don't you think, and sink to the marginal residue of our upkeep, if we don't have a theology to polish them with".[9] As such, he is then both sometime inhabitant and regular visitor to the place, creating a relationship out of which he can embark on an "interlinear commentary . . . threading questions and trials into the labyrinth, the complex displays of rock and vegetation, sheep-pens and graveyards . . ." (7). It was after she left for a life in London, that Presley began to return to and write regularly about her home area.

Wendy Mulford, in her preface to *The East Anglia Sequence*, talks about the "primary difference of context" between the first part of the sequence, written as a regular "visitor" to Salthouse, North Norfolk, and the second part, written as an "immigrant—or blow-in" to Dunwich, Suffolk.[10] Here is her description of the "visitor" approach:

What I was after in the Salthouse text was an encounter with other, experienced as/ located in the meteorology, archaeology, geology, ornithology, prehistory, the recorded history of place. The quick of it. The knowledge. (np)

I recognise this as similar to my own approach to West Cumbria when invited to write 'Particles' about a coast previously unknown to me. This is, in part, an acknowledgement of partial understanding, a degree of humility perhaps.

Mulford talks in more spiritualised terms when she writes about the second part of the sequence where she deepens both research and experience to "another 'real'", the "further tracking after what Buddhists call 'nowhere country', the place which is, finally, your home . . . retaining its profoundly resistant, unincorporated soul"(np). What is interesting about this description is that it reveals not a greater "knowledge" as one might expect from the sensitive settler, but an acceptance of place as ultimately inassimilable to human understanding. To write about a place where one has settled as an adult, whether it be the expatriate Tony Baker's France or my own West Yorkshire, is always to be discovering the knowable and unknowable, to be alive to its specificity.

When Riley writes of "The earth endlessly concealed" in the poem 'Vertigo', the shadow-word lurking behind "concealed" is surely "revealed". It is this revealing/concealing relationship between the human and the non-human worlds that radical landscape poetry explores. In Riley's 'Western States', he refers to the "mind beginning something/ out of nothing"—always a tricky companion. There is a tension about the fact that "Everything underfoot has a name", to cite Mulford's 'Goblin Combe'. At one level, it means it "matters like all grasses", but also that we have limited its specificity within our own meanings and the use it bears to us. This poetry is alive to the exploitative nature of all this history, this naming and ownership: "Nothing sells about this edge but fragrance", writes Macdonald in her cliff-edge poem, 'Dale'. Elisabeth Bletsoe's 'Pharmacopœia', her title evoking the history of drug-making from herbs, speculates on our relationship to plants. She refers throughout to the human usage of flowers, questioning the idea that this should be their sole purpose by widening our vision of each plant through reference to its multiple names, its places and conditions and its mythologies. Frances Presley's researches into stone circles and settings, pagan rites and goddess-worship flicker in and out of her poems. Her knowledge is worn lightly, fragmentarily, but adds to our sense of these places as mysterious in terms of their own existence and their social and religious history. In 'Human Remains and Sudden Movements', Davidson alludes repeatedly to the processes of archaeology, of literally getting beneath land, not as a simple act of discovery, but as a part of the palimpsest of humanity's long history of manipulation of landscape. The poems shifts fluidly between references to the natural features of the Anglesey coastline and the ancient and modern "human remains" that we see about us, from ruined chapels and burial sites to lighthouses and the building of new roads. This poetry is then, both rich in reference to the life of landscape now and full of traces of the past. The past, like the present, is explored both in terms of its greater honour and respect of nature as well as its exploitation and ruination. Often this palimpsesting of past and present sensibilities is literary or textual involving the citation of found text from diverse sources. Elisabeth Bletsoe's poetry is always in dialogue with historical texts, ranging from ancient herbals ('Pharmacopœia') to medieval book-paintings ('Birds of the Sherborne Missal') to nineteenth-century fiction (as in 'Cross-in-Hand' which re-visits Hardy's *Tess of the D'Urbervilles*). So Bletsoe multiplies her imaginative entrances into nature. There also seems to me to be an ecological element to this practice. The poet replaces the great romantic myth of originality, of the poet as a genius, with a more humble image of the poet as a re-user, a recycler of words, images and ideas. I am reminded of the poet Richard Caddel's chosen title for his selected poems, *Magpie Words* (Sheffield: West House Books, 2002). Contrary to popular belief, the best avant-garde poetries have always reached beyond inclusive self-referentiality. This practice acknowledges an important political and poetical principle, that there is not enough time for each generation to discover anew what words, philosophies and actions really matter.[11] It is not just literary analogy that we find in these texts, but also botanical, zoological and agricultural histories. So, Simms reflecting on the bonecaves of the North Pennines. So Riley's reference to "the old ridge-and-furrow system/ Striping the gently sloping dark/ green fields" in *Snow Has Settled [...] Bury Me Here*. So Mulford's historical references to floods and sea defences in the 'East Anglia Sequence', a poem in which local research feeds an exploration of an important global, environmental issue even as the lyric passages capture the sensual relationship to place.

bodies

Frances Presley's account of her emergence into landscape writing through a modernist poetic is a poignant one, echoed by women poets within and without this anthology.[12] Arguably, that journey is still ongoing, yet I was pleasingly surprised by the number of submissions to the special feature of the internet journal *How2* on Women and Ecopoetics I edited in 2007–8. Writing about the body in and of landscape is a particular strength of women poets, who have only relatively recently thrown off an objectified position as part of an idealised landscape in favour of a speaking one. Now we find male poets interested in the same territory. So Ian Davidson describes his own work as an attempt to "link the body to the landscape" and an exploration of "the way in which we read off the scale of our surroundings via the body".[13] In this anthology, the lure to the erotic in and of human and non-human nature can be read throughout from Johnson's "feet move: fern seeds/spill, buds across our sandals" to Skoulding's "The lines of the landscape/ run through me to somewhere else". Bletsoe's 'Pharmacopœia' is charged with the eroticism which can permeate our relationship to land and which I also explored in an early sequence, *Love/Land*. At the same time, her delicate, intricate poems draw on the traditional association of flowers with love and the sequence can also be read as a love story composed through flowers. Macdonald's pieces, such as 'Poem' and 'On approaching natural colours', dramatise the poet/land affair. Both end in emotive shifts in perspective on land. Perhaps the most obvious difference from traditional love poetry in a natural setting or using natural metaphors is that these lines are not humancentric. They are not only concerned with love between humans. Mark Dickinson writes:

One of the ways in which poetry functions within this paradoxical environment is to return to the body and to simply walk out into the world. By being in the world, through an intimacy of a thorough immersion, the poetry can radically re-engage with otherness and begin to propagate alternative ways of seeing and occupying place, or at the very least, remind us of the *intimacy* and *otherness* of our surroundings. Not by relocating the human body as the central process, but as a part of a process of being within and with the world.[14]

Dickinson's reference to walking here is important for many of these poets for whom the "Where, Why and etcetera" of walking is how the writing happens (Macdonald). "[M]otion is the natural mode of human and animal vision: 'We must perceive in order to move <u>but we must also move in order to perceive</u>'", writes Pierre Joris, citing James J. Gibson's, *The Ecological Approach to Vision Perception*.[15] This idea then of (re)-entering the body leads us to consider our mammalian nature. The relationship between the human and the non-human is a major debate within ecological circles and one which contemporary poets, Maggie O'Sullivan and Colin Simms being perhaps the most notable examples, also explore.[16]

In this anthology we find some striking examples of poetry which engages with our fellow-creatures. Simms' 'Carcajou: A Poem of Encounter' is a rich and honest piece, sometimes witty, sometimes frightening, but always challenging. As Simms writes, "it's a fallacy of our time that our 'knowledge' has us understand". He explores other ways of "encounter", raising the question of the degree to which we are or are not animal and the degree to which we can and cannot relate to non-human beings, and they to us. I hope the reader will seek the full poem. Similarly, I am able to include only a few fragments of Simm's *Otters and Martens* poems, selected from his book-length text, the culmination of over thirty years of observation and writing about these creatures. Although, in form and technique, Simms and Macdonald are very different poets, in philosophy and feeling their bird poems confront us with the same radical attempt to enter that shift between sky-view and earth-view, the spun contrasts between "northern-lights" and "catseyes" chimed together in the final "blink" of Simms' 'Snowy Owl, for Laura'.

More recent poems published here, such as Mark Goodwin's 'Dark Bird With Corner' and Helen Macdonald's 'Skipper/copper', continue to attempt animal encounter with cautious integrity. In 'Skipper/copper', Macdonald moves vertiginously between scales: the "living creature" hanging over a marsh one second and leaving a little dust on a human hand the next. She goes on to set the worth of a butterfly's death ("Who cares if it flies again/ flying things/ dumb objects which flinch and fall again") against the metaphorical worth of the fall of the butterfly to the poet. The reader is left feeling complicit in human lack of care or even knowledge of the objectified creature, skipper or copper. We do not even know.[17]

Finally, as I hope I have shown here, it is not just the poet in landscape, but the place of humanity in landscape that is at the heart of this work, what Frances Presley has called a "peopled landscape".[18]

Presley's voices include not just the people in her life at the time of writing ("Kelvin said/ Just the sea Frances"), but a wider collection of found voices. This is echoed throughout this collection, Here, there are many people, members of communities that still cling on in this country and who have value in the eyes of these poets: the casual observers scattered throughout Baker's 'aurals', the farming voices in Watts' 'Zeta Landscape', the scrap-metal collectors in my own 'Particles'. From another ecological viewpoint, of course it is people that are the problem. This is the great, often unspoken, crisis of over-population, and that too is touched on here. Through his probing philosophical work, sometimes gentle, sometimes brutal, Peter Larkin sets the idea of scarcity against the idea of teeming. In 'Open Woods', with reference to human clearing and inhabitation of land, he poses the question: "No one is saying it wrong in human concentrates, but how ubiquitous should be the teem?" In stark contrast, Clark's work, with the use of the vocative case, leads or invites us into a very different response to the rapacity and ubiquity of humanity. He suggests it might be possible to carve out a quiet space for an unobtrusive human presence in nature and traces delicate shifts in experience:

> the hill that was dark
> is now bright
> imperceptibly sensation
> glows to emotion
> then fades again

Notes

[1] The pages also relate to Presley's delvings into the archaeological work of the forgotten Exmoor writer, Hazel Eardley-Wilmot, as I discuss the in greater depth in 'Recycles: the Eco-Ethical Poetics of Found Text in Contemporary Poetry' in the *Journal of Ecocriticism* Vol. 1: No.2 (2009) http://ojs.unbc.ca/index.php/joe/issue/view/17

[2] Bunting, Basil, *Collected Poems*, Oxford and New York: Oxford University Press, 1977, 54

[3] This is a somewhat simplified summary of the introductory paragraph of Larkin's 'Fully From, All Scarce To' in Iijima, Brenda. *)((Eco(Lang)(uage(Reader))*, Brooklyn, New York: Portable Press at Yo-Yo Labs and Callicoon, New York: Nightboat Books, 2010. A useful book, though Larkin is the only British poet featured.

[4] See Tarlo, 'Radical Landscapes: experiment and environment in contemporary poetry' *Jacket* 32 (April 2007), http://jacketmagazine.com/32/index.shtml and Tarlo, Harriet 'Women and Ecopoetics: An introduction in Context', special feature on ecopoetics *How2* Vol 3: No 2 (2008) http://www.asu.edu/pipercwcenter/how2journal/vol_3_no_2/index.html

[5] Skinner, Jonathan, ed. *ecopoetics* http://www.factoryschool.org/ecopoetics/, a valuable resource.

[6] Watts has written about the process of writing Zeta Landscape in *Poetry Wales* 45.3 (Winter 09/10).

[7] Garrard, Greg, *Ecocriticism*, London: Routledge, 2004, 56.

[8] In a preview of this anthology prepared for *English* magazine in 2009 I discuss in greater detail the intricacies of the terms, landscape poetry, pastoral poetry, ecopoetry and ecopoetics. In this introduction I prefer to talk more about the work itself.

[9] Riley, Peter (1995) Preface, *Alstonefield,* London and Plymouth: Oasis/Shearsman, 7.

[10] Mulford, Wendy (1998) Preface, *The East Anglia Sequence: Norfolk 1984–Suffolk 1994*, Peterborough, Cambs: Spectacular Diseases.

[11] This argument is itself recycled from my own essay on 'Recycles: the Eco-Ethical Poetics of Found Text in Contemporary Poetry' in the online *Journal of Ecocriticism* Vol. 1: No.2 (2009) http://ojs.unbc.ca/index.php/joe/issue/view/17

[12] Presley, Frances, 'Common Pink Metaphor: from The Landscape Room to Somerset Letters', *How2* Vol 3: No 2 (2008) http://www.asu.edu/pipercwcenter/how2journal/vol_3_no_2/index.html

[13] 'Afterword', *At a Stretch,* Shearsman Books, 2004, 109.

[14] Mark Dickinson, 'Peter Larkin's Knowledge of Place', *Cordite Poetry Review* http://www.cordite.org.au/features/mark-dickinson-peter-larkins-knowledge-of-place#_ftn2_2965

[15] Gibson, James J. *The Ecological Aproach to Vision Perception* (1986). Hillsdale, NJ and London: Lawrence Erlbaum Associates Publishers; Joris, Pierre. *A Nomad Poetics: Essays* (2003). Middletown, CT: Wesleyan University Press.

[16] Sadly, O'Sullivan was the only poet asked who did not want to be included the anthology.

[17] Macdonald has also written prose texts about birds of prey. Her blog, http://fretmarks.blogspot.com/2007/06/sprawks-and-thoughts.html, includes some spectacular writing about flying hawks, an interesting complement to her poetry.

[18] Presley, Frances, Interview with Edmund Hardy. *Intercapillary Space* (Oct. 2006) at http://intercapillaryspace.blogspot.com/2006/10/interview-with-frances-presley.html. This tendency is also evident in her collaborative projects, particularly her site specific work with the poet and textual artist, Tilla Brading.

In memory of three poets of the North East whose work explored land, place and locality, and who died too young:

Barry MacSweeney (1948–2000)

> . . . my heather-crashing feet, splash happy
> kneefalls along the tumblestones,
> whip-winged plovers shattering the dew

> (from 'Pearl')

Bill Griffiths (1948–2007)

foot	stamen	finger	coin	beak	vertebra
pistil	penis	mandible	petal	proboscis	ungulate
hair	pollen	cornet	button	sceptre	horn
claw	trumpet	trunk	barbule	operculum	star-point

(from 'Fragments: A History of the Solar System')

Richard Caddel (1949–2003)

Lichen days
light   a
        history—

I have seen the hills, and they were just the hills
I faced into the wind, it blew on me

rest there–

> (from 'Little Stringer')

COLIN SIMMS

Snowy Owl, *for Laura*

Lift
strength
detachable   as if snow carded itself

                                        nothing stealth
                                        nothing else

                               for fold to hold barred-bold bird
dismissible deal below   white the world spins hardheard
shuffling cards coils diamonds dull white cools clubs spades coals real-slack glow
grow stars more starkly sparkle   eyes between us swivel slowly slow
presence here farmfence formless-force   as yet combs muskeg beyond
pure shawl an owl; so across space out of it!
full of owl; so right northern-lights vane
catseyes at home on the road at night   blink

January 1976

The Crags at Crookleth Beacon

for E.Z. and Ezra and E.K.

man-and-boy   mischief chuckles

Jacks   reverse   beckon   chacks   from nest-cracks
shun   new hooligan - with - the - gun   boycott new-come cottagers
shock rock-chimney stacks   bring back chiding children, nutcracking

On High Crosset Climbers Comb
                    an hour destroys the kestrels' home, charnel-tower

their privacy-plucked piracy   *ching*   chine-sing from chinks, in clints
sheep merely shear,   shift stints   will   goes   when   people   hit   the   hill.

Prairie wheatfield had been prairie buffalo-grass-land   before soddies and sodcutters
the birds remain   Meadowlarks sing longitude   morning and evening   only
in heat-of-the-day   in the fence-shade

                                                    the long refrain
Horned-larks spiral song   weedseed-feed no rain   early afternoon
                                    black vee
                            ripe for skylarks   with this kind of cultivation
            the new land is   never mind the economics of the trip

                        give me a poetry of observed relationship

from **Carcajou**

who can face encounter   who must face it
listen in the forest first where the voices we want to hear
are not people's but of The People   In uit
                              made
                        out of the glade
enlightenment is sudden in the forest   eyes bright-red-brown-as-Mars
star for further looking level looking-in intermittent contact had been interment
you, Carcajou, only just recognised and before we know you
                                            we listen for a tune
to engage being out-of-sight so much we require a ritual for a fitting-in
                  Dutilleux' *Symphonic Fragments*, fragmented
Le Loup might be so augmented
                        where you will be in our imagined-scheme-of-things
not hibernating, but we stop looking for light in the dark place we are in
the American dream-blight quick through every sensuous delight   active day or night
experiencing everything in a hurry   ahead of itself   the Fright
"omnivorous, the wolverine"   our starting place the Given Word
before we know its prejudice   Are you bear or weasel, wolverine,
or both   the space between your eyes is wide,   we all
to shallow graves you can grub up   Ours, are the animals—
      evolution is the space between true trees
                  What kind of animal would you have been?
Trust starts at the eyes
timing   and works in
what is there   there   who ever does a bad thing, it is bad:
                              to make the word good
                              theres something animal in all of us
                              and a different animal is everyone
people and animals relate,   its one way into them for us,   and it must be for them also
                        one hero is one who
exposes himself where others watch, the only one willing to go forward for good
for others

[. . .]

23

reaching beyond the visible
and all that takes our mind off what-goes-on.   The forest floor we walk on
carries all signature heavy self-consciousness "clawed, *vicious*"
(Don't look at me, for my forté   is taking animals out of other mens traps)
The first words in   having been in traps myself I'm through with them
until the next one
                    This is a wood you increase by coming-out-of-it—
                    out into the snow with a sawing motion of it—
bear-lope   muskrat-ramble   badger-trundle   marten-amble
                              the evolution we are in
is secondary-skin   concerned to sensitivity
with texture and with feel   the ritual further is
if you go, and with assent   (not to interfere)   the mustelidae exist
insist Rilke was wrong: you can point out a scent, weasels exist by this
not so much stealth in the stoop or the chase or the pounce   but persistence
quiet, laced there is taste in scent   stands on end when incensed
"consistent, lank, rather rough but generous"   this, of the fur
showing a little out of the forest   essential nature is in skin
                    coming across to meet my   nervousness:–
an animal with a Tertiary look about it, somewhat unspecialised
                              individual and geographic variation
                              Celt-oval-headed, wide
forehead and wide walk; the eyes wide apart, the giant marten
the genes a long time rearing in the same pattern of creation
as the Giant Ground Sloth Darwin found; the Megatherium
something of it in the nature of the fur; Änne as if in the accent on her hair
stationary, evolutionary as stone : bones   rare, old, peculier!
an animal swinging in off the ground, never off the trees
                                        the mere idea of you

back-of-the-mind and building-over for years: on the wind the scent of you
so that eventually, after inactivity   out to the place logistics have suggested
          the game
so that eventually, after uncertainty, lame, rested in it;   we move, against the grain
          a name   just one species

Mustela barbata, viverra vittata, Taira mustela, Mustela gulo, Gulo gulo
Gulo luscus, Cub hylaeus, Gubo luteus, Cub biedermanni, Cub wachei,
Cub katschemakensis, Gulo bairdi, Gulo niedecki, Gubo auduboni.

[. . .]

To be here at all now, to be here anyway
the animal has adapted to a thousand different niches
competing with wolves   bears   (including polar bears)
      fishers   —they are already their own giant-martens
      martens   (and so, sables)   foxes
      arctic foxes   golden eagles   great owls, what else . . .
the big wind and out of it   it brings you, it is what brings you
on its noise out of the sticks   which makes you coming   But it is not you.
The wind is you past and the grasses settling again because of you, brushing
them wider, lower, harder than the badger;   and the trees are narrower, you brashing.
You are the racks in the forest and in the ice, the rhythm-tension that the wind
can only speak of even when it is breaking trees.
You have been, in your momentum over millenia the centre bearing down
the direct confrontation at approaching speed, head down
a blur, the line direct and straight-at-me.
You have been the difference between being right up to my insides, and distant
but not silent in the forest;   no, not that
or out of sight.   You are in the flourish, the stripe of speed along your side
you have been everything I have not known but in longer moments than expected:
a response
My questions, you say, have always had different levels;
the real issue so sudden and direct
it takes the breathaway.

[. . .]

Carcajou, it is you
rimming forest a long ridges I've been all the day   but night comes slow
emptier of heart than cold coming-on-my-way   the forest/voices low
moan   I would not say alone
        feeling the light only penetrate
sawing away, chewing. I am a chainsaw of the woods that you   can sing,
cant see me through : its the co-operation thats coming in nature, I grant you
Rilke is wrong; you can point out a scent   Enlightenment is man and caribou
          mouse and Carcajou
      we of the weasel family survive by this:
there is a taste in scent   stands on end when incensed

persistence, quiet   (not just letting light in):
the wind does that from time to time on its own helped out in winter by an extra weight of snow
there is the certain rhythm comes in before you do (not just letting sap run):
the sun itself, forgotten for a while, with a little help from scratching badgers if the spring will come
       consistent, lank, rather rough, but generous
(this of the fur) merely a naturalist's description.   Not just opening minds:
like a thaw lifting blinds for chords and cords to saw   opening the minds
your way is just leading timber away   education is more than that.
    needing   naturally, nationality   has nothing to do with it
it is the place we are, whether we find it   neither near nor far whether we mind it
    imagination   (what figure, grimmer, than Grimm's Woodcutter)
    the release I feel is your
(conscious of it are you or unconscious?)   penetration
    the old world figure of organisation   the ring I walk is yours
enlightenment isnt just letting light in   in the clearing
    the wind does that from time to time
    I am for you this moment if you can take it :–
    on its own
(or helped in winter by the extra weight of snow)
    prairie-sage to no old-age,
    not just letting sap run
dance to the sun this sundew, dance :   the sun itself, forgotten for a while
    the babes in the wood would, if they could   (with a little help
from scratching squirrels, badgers, vibrating sap-suckers   when the spring will come
    watchout for wolf lest carcajou get you
    not just even   opening minds
    like a thaw lifting blinds for chords to soar
    imagination   and not tradition
the old world fairy-tale organisation   in imagination what figure is Grimmer
than Grimm's Woodcutter   against wolf and wilderness cutting trees down over a continent
and then over another: watchout for wolf lest Carcajou catch you!

The land says   to decide
this scrap tin has had time   in gullies and in ditches—
since this land was made-over to decide   old cars are hard to hide
second-generation mechanician I am   not the indigene
that from the beginning was like this, adaptable   the so-called   Indian
whose trail we all must find   I sit a metal ridrind
rust and laugh (you've seen the oxidised stripe on my side!)
    laugh-grind

you wont find me here!

                       what you do   is look in the wrong places
       for luck   Carcajou,
After the Explorer

          you run on old trails, unquestioning
After the Exploiter

          you are left still unknown   and unknowing
After the Organiser

          you are anarchy   "My Teeth Make New"
After the Hunter

            and you only name a few though he is all of you
      I am still chewing through true, too
After the conservator   I am uncatered for, still
the eyes, and back-of-the-eyes, spell naked for what a lens would not tell
or dispel, but enlarge illusion on leaving like wanting to touch sway hips
the coat, the rank fur's thousand lips,   the points of the electric snow on them
show great stoat not naked fur
an exchange of saliva groomed across a distance   the cord running through,
the thread has its insulation before ignition or it is earthed:
to make a start, a stand, we cautiously declare to share the land
its a fallacy of our time that our 'knowledge' has us understand
so we can 'automatically' communicate, co-operate.   Carcajou, its not true
we are no more investing than inventing the situation, I'm not making you:
whatever it is we can say, differently, together, do and go along with
each in his and her own space and place so to be with it, strong with
its own reality, not its own image or abstraction, changing and sense
in the beginning a place-recognition, we realise after growing commonsense
in time and in tune I'll learn from the 'animal' and which is you—
what we make in our heads that is not new, never can be even, true
whatever it is called.   Encounter before imagination is in you, Carcajou.

Otter Dead in Water (Drowned by 'keeper) 1984

Watter had vitalled   nourished, gi'en blood
that wettens now   wattles and muddied
blood leif to leave   of its pressure
treasured and swelled   smells .... unhurried
as taints in current   spraints meshed and measured
air over the river   arrested   even stones
so they grow green-ness   as his muzzle will, heedless
by the same stones marked   where the flood reached the moon
blood leased by leeches   stone-loaches the otter ett
long passion decides   where floodwater subsides
length and strength   and tides

Loch Maree 1970

lochside silverschistsand disturbed-to-black-below distributed
pattern-padded pewter-grade velvet-hollows grains added otter pattern
wind off water levelling sibilant bevelling gritscreen bankscree
whistle   reminding you of   distant wigeon whee-oo
lifting, see prints between bents-tail-race-slice-silt sift sting
still tracks slow upslope shorten portage not forage but for ages
we newcomers can begin to see pattern   even from this little elevation
braids loosen elements-stream raise islands   bruised-
petal-heartsease-violet trail wakes prospect of please not violence
increasing-in-confidence   bolder heavier just before lost in boulders

        when we were least aware the stiff log dogging windshore
sure-of-his-lie breaks cover sure-of-his-line leans lie of the land over
from under could not-have-hidden-him right-under-feet wonder
instead left-right losing-using his whole enters not-in-the-line-of-his-head
twisting quick long into the river's plaited-in on-itself longitudinal as time
otters were here before
might be   but rivers were like that
if there is still any life in them

bonecave, North Pennines 1969

       dibble out a mandible tight   in   stalactite
badger it loose carefully   prized or might-be-otter
compare   osteologically   to be fair
the weasel-family   share   some structure

concerned to discover what-comes-up-from-a-place
hard impressions to put flesh on   lines-to-a-face

but we don't know individual-behaviour-same-stricture
what river-otters were *doing*
to be interred in high-ridge caves   even in human burial-cysts
      an accidental   en-fracture
      what when these high-dry hills were not
high dry hills but
so "what does it tell you   what is it worth"
decent-clearing-events of small patch of an old earth.

Scargill Otter

Horizons range as you climb north from Deepdale Beck
aligned yet continuous (at your level, what?) above Deepdale (the) wreck
—line of limestone   like its reefs   sails reefed in/by
ragline of buildings.   Kine   farms and barns
their dykes and walls and swales and little rises   of old usage
nature outcrops   backsapping likes   itself; it repeats
or is in emphasis   (not denial)   it repeats itself
that is, : its nature and feature

PETER RILEY

Prelude

Snow has settled in the lines
Of an old ridge-and-furrow system
Striping the gently sloping dark
Green fields, engrossed script
Of duration, repetition, authority
At which that calm baby in the self
That finds it so difficult to speak
Lowers an eyelid on the shrinking day
And suddenly says outright
The entire brochure of love and all.
Stay here before you fall.

from The Llŷn Writings

Porth Grwtheyrn, 21st August 1985

Yellow poppy, groundsel, carlin thistle,
Tangles of metal rope, rusted iron cogwheels
Sunk in sand. Slate, granite, aggregate, shale.
Flung wiremesh, rails, bolts, rivets, grills,
Axle, roller, valve, beam, plate.
Rustle of water down cliff-face. Hawk, goat,
Wild shore strewn with lumps of concrete.
Mermaid's purse, crab-shell, sandhoppers, boat.
Plastic bottles, rope knots, tin cans, bird bones.
Oystercatcher, little gull, wave smacks gravel.
My hair a thin cushion against the stones.
Concrete telegraph hut, bits of copper cable
Still dangling from it. Monster ruin of loading quays.
My family, my lunch, my erratic, growling days.

from A Map of Faring

Open land, then forest, then air.

Leonardo Bruni said that the harmonious
workings of the institutions of Florence
derived from the beauty and geometry
of the Tuscan landscape.

A thin track, a line in the grass across
the pastures and over the riverside humps
everywhere worked, the shape of the place
carved from work, lines curving to meet,
leading ultimately homewards.

Roofwatch (1)

Day and night the sky arches over
hills and plain turning against
the earth, clouds springing
from the dark wooded edge fan
over the farmed land and at
night the plethora of stars
turns clear and sure and
compact in their terraces
above a veiled and separated ground.
O fine in their farming the stars
rally and exit all night.

The Walk to Roussillon

The red cliff in the dark green woods,
walk towards it. As you get
closer it is difficult to see.

Vertigo

Moving out of the tree border into the top grasslands.
This is the earth, and this is us here very close to it,
watching the great valley below, everything clinging to the ground
small black ants on my arm butterflies in pairs in the grass
I'm working on a statement of political hatred black
flies gentle breeze clinging to the hillside carrying
a few birds down below, shirt patched with sweat
drying to salt lines, chilled skin. Faint wood smoke
in the crowded breeze cow bells among the trees
and an iridescent green spider. Seeking in this thronging
vocabulary to think a clear thought about human wrong
which does not disown us. Deceits practised within
necessity. Deceits of the grassy bank. Small
shepherds' huts all over the slopes, secretive hiss
of wind through larches endless forest and mountain
and clouded sky over all, over the oil plants and
railway sidings beside which people survive regimes and
rebellions with luck and custom. Cockchafer climbing
a grass stem, yellow vetch clusters, the earth
written in black ink, hidden under the fuel.

The earth endlessly concealed. Larch top horizons
followed down into the black haze under the mountainside
or the caterpillar's back: the great void of images,
the thought pit, fires glowing in it. Down there
we inhabit this darkness and harvest this blue wheat.
The limestone subsoil that smelts up saxifrage and self-heal.

Harecops

Grace and honour
descend the hill

Seeking the human heart
brushing aside the wasps

And folding that knotted
academy in clay hands . . .

•

Our front window looked out two
miles over pasture and woodlands thick
with the sheen of equity, that eschews
greed or fantasy, its pale emblems still
shelved at the field edges and tending
to fade into the ground. We held on
to this optimism. We sank our trust in
curtained arbours of a stone house
and formed a child, who guided us
through the dark shops.

•

And two miles away was a great ridge,
a dark green mass strung with white stone walls

At its highest point an ancestral grave,
a circular fate calendar of long stones.

When we looked through the window it was
always there, though the light came and went.

White stone messengers
pierced the night and

Focused the day, calling
to the mind, to the cupped heart,

Calling together the kind forces
that hunt us to death.

from **Shining Cliff**

December, patches of bracken stalks
brown leaves clinging to some of the trees
and strewn in the pale grass, thousands
of chestnuts rotting on the ground

The A6, slightly visible, slightly audible
down the end of the valley through the trees
your route home to southern business.
Remember this north before its bitterness:

Hairclips, Cuban rap, analysis
And a farewell to the song thrush.

from **Alstonefield**

The mountain edge barely clears, folded back.
Surface that is a line hanging in the air
at which sight withdraws, a clarity on paper
anterior to the earth, broken by ink.
Lines that converge without touching
open centrally to a linen distance,
the whole air a time table. Light from
the blade retires behind the hill at
a slight flexing of the globe as the words
I thought this with fly to your calvarium.

I walk back to Beresford in the afternoon.
The coal tit, dyed in modern philosophy,
flits for nuts. Snow on the shoulder, sky
narrowed between hill and hill a blue-grey
tongue for any speech is distant at the time.
Silence lines the horizon, glowing to a lost
nation, snow-brushed fields glossing the vein
to a hole in tense, a history of light
or moving pain to paper an agreement is touched,
that death shall have no choice.

from **Western States**

5

Distant ridges dim in haze, stone under foot, red
and grey the book of emptiness, the final prize

8

Red ink on the sides of the canyon, Navajo script
and the great emptying, the great advance

9

We turn our backs and the deer
come to drink in the dark

11

The wind that comes hissing over the white rock
of Carmel, the white friars

begging in the desert
lighter than the sky

47

The end of the road in a scatter of grey bushes
mind beginning something

out of nothing, in nowhere, turning
towards life, pale stony ground

48
Empty mind turns looks
around sees the real

"land without people"
and fills with bitterness

low grey bushes with yellow flowers
breathe in and breathe out

49
To see so far and see nothing in the distance
the rubbish-tip you thought was called life

50
Vast fields of silence
in the distance the sound of distance

miserable assumptions
prisons and nuclear waste

52
Small low sand humps showing
marks of lizards' and birds' feet

and sometimes the streak of a tail, delicate
engravings on barely compacted ground

53
The mind completely distinct, dark and sharp edged
turns to command the desert sky

where concrete apertures
shelter the new tribes

Thomas A Clark

The Grey Fold

lifting your eyes
take the small voyage
out to the horizon
and back again

along the high water mark
of the strandline
in a storm of sand grains
drenched in salt spray
bound in a mesh of roots
between the foredune
and the yellow dune
between loss and consolidation
in the hollow of the dune slack

you are the one
walking alone
intermediary between
earth and sky

a delicate yellow
prepared by green
nourished on rock
in a salt wind

tenuous at first
then tentative
always hesitant
reticent later

the hint
of a touch
of colour
on a branch

the suggestion
of a breath
of warmth
in the air

between gorse
and coltsfoot
the yellowhammer

between coltsfoot
and gorse
the yellowhammer

there is a mist
in the light
that is of the light
and not of air
or water

that which you touch
steps back
the impossible flower
the immediate
at arm's length
under your fingertips

an astonishment
prolonged
as if it were raining
stillness

only when you stop
and sit for a while
among the wild hyacinths
do you know where desire
was leading you

on a stone beside water
listening to the water
and to something else
serious and delicate
playing behind the sounds

on its bed of moss
the fern is a form
that draws the eye
across a complex space
as if the moss had made
within complexity
space for a form

the hill that was dark
is now bright
imperceptibly sensation
glows to emotion
then fades again

with measured steps
with deliberation
walk the quiet path
the between time
the grey fold

WENDY MULFORD

Goblin Combe

Everything underfoot has a name. Is named. Each
anonymous grass, moss repeats a history how
long the path who walked it what used to grow when
disturbance came—that's
dog's mercury the only exciting thing about
it comes early.
From a distance of several hundred yards at a speed of 70 mph
it's a matter of attention
& memory—in this quiet
the pine cones pop raggedly
woodpecker suns so soft so distant so distinct I daren't think
in the steep always damp of the gorge-cleft
the violet-bunch clinging at the rockface wild
garlic & uprooted hellebore—
such richness is & light why do our days stony?
To vow not is to remember &
that matters like all grasses.

Composed 1970s

from **The East Anglia Sequence** *(revised version)*

Salthouse 1099, 1953

'At Martinmas the incoming tide rushed up so strongly that none
remembered the like before'.

> A lot of redbreasted flycatchers
> "Ich bin Brahms, Doktor Johannes Brahms"
> the high clear-pane windows transmit
> light from north to south from west to east
> shut the doors or the sound will die
> under the plain timber roof no glories
> of angels no chancel mysteries
> wood stone tiles for your seafaring people
> the sea washes through like light

The cost of protection would be out of proportion
to the value of the limited land area protected:
by the time the sea-bank goes the worst will be over—
approximately 40% of the houses are empty much of the year—
it would be cheaper to buy up all the properties at risk
than to spend £500,000 on sea defences

> hedges tall & plump with berries
> hips sloes elder slide off
> drop in delayed harvest
> sea-lavender faded heather gorse
> burning slow crab-
> bodies track the marsh worn worm-
> coils tile the pools oyster-
> catchers scratch the air
>
> beyond palings beyond bridges
> where settlement and sea contend

Voices 1986

SHIP-BREAKING
MARINE & RECOVERY WORK
WRECKS DISPOSED OF
SPARE PARTS SALVAGED

No change can make anyone better off without simultaneously making
someone

At the quarters of the moon severally, 12:17, 2:52, 4:39, 3:02
The spring tide at the full moon
nine feet two
at the full moon this year

& every year, the moon-pull
irresistibly, fatly, hungrily
always, flowing to the moon
(plant your boots) hungrily
richly, inexorably
overswayed

worse off

Samphire, thrift
S
amphire, thrift, sea-aster,
S
alicornia, zostera,
E
el-grass, sea-
L
avender, shrubby sea blite
T
he sea nourishes & cleanses
T

wice daily its huswifely scavenging
S
couring succouring unable
T
a let be bygone filters snitches back
D
eposits scraped into rivulets & channels
T
he sea seeding its self own bed

Salthouse, 1986

In a rusty shed
caressing the long lines
the sharpee's
rusty owner
fingertip tenderly
touch through centuries
carved seas
the new men
lean back

In converted barns
blow-ins lament
Money's incandescent
braying from bar-stools
the fishing-fleet smothers
meadows ploughed up
nitrogen pools

The condition of paradise is loss
on a shrinking coast
when you can't afford
auctioned solitude or
the steep subscription for the
orchid tamped with officious
solicitude & creatureliness
retreats
leaving the land to new leisure

Sea's measure

S
ea's measure reassuring
L
andedness ends
B
oundary to earth's flap
E
quivocation
S
pring summer winter
S
ea-storm or calm
L
andfarer's last line to vision
D
rawn off the map —

Whose voice this is
beneath the shoals beneath the over
falls the knocks imperfectly
surveyed the outer dowsing unreliable
wrecks omit the ambiguity of depth

from CODA

A Tale of Loss

1
now her an
april snow
in november hurt dry wind
confusion whipping away
light soil gritting
eyes lips soiled
sneak under
touch
melting the sea
       breached the honeycomb
       base & how do you
       face trust erosion

in the loss of the
as certainty
blunts the mind print
blunts the imagination

2
gold hard lithe hard leaps shadow-ward
a torn pole striking out a spar across the
dirty ocean of
loss yes off course loveliness
tall backed straight skyward dropping
off the page aureole glory hard
glowing toes point back to
earth hammered
whips irradiate

3

it's warm june now sudden to
caress and drowsing light silken space
heavy-headed hanging nod sweet silence
trips hairline touch the flowers
still the dune edge the shacks
sleep the street snoring
grey friars till the almighty's swipe
the coast crumpled

gentle dalliance as
lips broken-backed this
tide's recurring pattern who's
to place and law unbroken can you

sweep all before as
lights ride out the night
close eyes to dream then navigate
to open ebb impassable
you enter harbour on the flood

5

bark gleams space fretted woodily
looped with travelling clouds their journey make
& through chords of rooks & pheasant barks the
piping plunging curlew wail of sirens are
as timpani to play
heraldry with winter light

I'm in my car or at my table. hum
drum. in each
particularity
stone-crop tile massed
orchard spikes in exile of
becoming

if brightness is winged and possible that theme declares
percussively before
submitting doubt to query
nudging across a pale palette a note
unrecognised
the rest is settlement beneath the hand

point to the rising moon
as toes to earth

6
there's cold in the heart but you could stop it
don't make believe
stand on your head you cannot rage
soles spread to the eagle sky

divinity, what is
heaven is it haven
to lose the harbour is one night's work
or slower
tempests take up a
lifetime's tacking to lie
in calm water all currents devious deep
driving or
air upstead currents breathing, insteps spread to
sun's balm
dream the poisoned source
renew

point to the rising moon
as toes to earth

can rush in the lungs forgotten with illicit knowledge
air and divinitie that here-and-now to heal in hope with
in without come gliding under first
star-sign moth-print bat-bless as petals silently
close float the panoply of nippies the sky's azure paling
across the rush white sailtops soundless brush the galaxy oh hear me out

Composed 1984–1994

from Alltud: 'exile'

In the valley of the Wye, Erwood, Powys

    birdsong.   peopletalk. sleepchatter.
   a dot grows visible like the bad monk beneath the abba's habit
    stumbling from the dark amphora into the strangeness of light
   a little light at dusk by which to sit and read the blanched white ash-stems reaching sky
    ward the steep woody tangle above the tumbling stream each stem gleams in the January dull
   every thing is still   except the invisible water thrashing over the weir & somewhere,
   the pulsing throats of songbirds
   wheels within wheels within wheels this one woody watery day fading—the thickness,
   the weave & baffle of it the fit between root and bird and rock and silt and rushing water
   the separate equilibration in each material bed and how jammed together plant and bird
   and human, fish and mammal
    the dart of tree-creeper salmon-leap into still pool froth & jetsam snagged
on ledges
    human   detritus
     there's just the darkening light blurring the mountain-back   the water stonily downward
   the gleaming ash-stems against a rubbed- out strip of sky closing the steep valley sides
    a sudden lift   breath passes from stem to branch to twig   minipassacaglia slowbeats
   and turns and animates gathering strength the
   casement pane bangs
  hush the chatter
  creatures of stardust   intent on meaning   stare

Composed 2007

December — Anemone rising

Frost. the
post and rails
slippery. the pond
dark. at the edge
of the clearing the modern
charcoal-burner sits
over black
smoke rising.   rubber
dioxins.   how we trash our
circumambient beauty.
meanwhile the purple anemone
raises its head
to salute the sun —
it can no more stop rising than we
reinventing ourselves

Composed 2008/9

PETER LARKIN

from Slights Agreeing Trees

Turf Hill

Some livery to simplify a real shank through the wards, power-lines at a slope of conduction with rapid incomplete owing of ground. To blow with spreading on the grid some green flutter of smaller rigid body.

Not covert and long not to be covered in links of shadow, a joined way lifts itself into fringe. The pylon avenue isn't corridor pulse interceding with plantation, but ventilation as if by air-arc of the horizons within clump. To displenish beside refreshed ground, what is healed and hugs shaft but never swings anew upon line-break. Grit at the big branch, anti-tentacular of hung community, but generously ferned.

How the boles thin to the widener of tracking turf, pylon by terrace of heeded instrument! If the tree-standing for wire is the pull of cantileaf, what can indent its continuous ornament looping on power-line? The trees are resident by unavailing advantage, full technical sorrow lattices their derivative store of staying beside-hand a cloaked way below. Each wafer strut as actuator, soft spring between wing and store. Field follower across overhead pitch, into the straits which fertilise a neb of impasse, but where wire cups to its beak a lift of towers inciting local spine, so spike your green along. Forked untransformable at heel of branch, trees topped for their sail-at-root, they bare these iron masts whenever nothing can have happened to the great limb.

Penned to place browsing rubric at passover, a hangar of unmixed trees is to the very source so little absorbent of archaic refuels off line. The pylon position anterior to ground raiment they are the plantings beside. These graces rest from detail, a culvert where timber narrows from indigenous refuge, crossed by splint of site-renewal, but always beneath a mono-difference which is for cable the single swoop other, inelastic divergence along towers. The trees perform the alterity at a remove which decreases into their own, derivatives at an unmoving dispersal. A current which tilts but levels out effect shorn upright at each organic corner. Overhang (below) steers to an angle shady with branched case of the relay, delicate tips hardly shamble a temple of greenest cages on stake-by. Or seed initiative to the more *consultant* rigidity, parapet of a tree's outwired profile.

Confession to gantry is pure-pining for a fabric of previous limb, cut to sidings of nonhuman repetition (stable remission), given a tower-split to land on. Meanwhile, the trees compare obedience to this graph of the open hearth, its free hollow is heath across them, with what remains of their own nape of verticals prised towards porous tier. Sigh for morphous readiness, precariously inactive by what discerns the infill. How easy the open is, cut commonly to infinite row! It coats the plantation's corridor with escape-stint primaries, attachable outward healing alarm in green.

Rising margin cocoons a planted oblivion, the landlight of surge fosters a dawning onto apron stake, conductors made nonspecular or no backing for tintless trees. Light can do nothing with this holster of woodland, keep it drawn to nurture only where it was outmarched. If denuded to a sentry of passage, still the pent tenantry of spending tracery like iron branch or root.

How trees stand ajar-remote at their reparation schedules. Sitedly gapped, no use-of-passage goes to unless it be their misassembly apart. Incompressible flow knows the studded circuitry of tree load. Detection of infill is raking the conduit, flash-overs of insulation are stroked transversely by the branches' own shield cable.

The tree like a cradle of wire has no pylon-pause for the elevation. These superstrings awake the wood cord, bake over it. Braced for the inexhaustions of line, insular cup these greener slots sip, shade slipped through needle. New wood transfixed by a peremptory earth's infused tower. Swathed forest interval roped aloof by the kilter of interruption. If this, too, composes arenas of completion, the savings were too unwandering for there to be any linear invective against inclusion.

Wire sag falters no crossings, increases fibrous entreaty by way of its attrition not entering but swelling out shelter. Root means square error for non-linearity, cross-stalk, or drift with no output other than put biding the contraction below-mast. The hazard is trees pose no traditional housings, unhidden by brilliant conduction of own limiters. This secondary panning to pylon is unintervening, a leaf away from mutilated ground.

Seedling pine caught gridded onto relational scatter, lean lid for bare earth, fraught with the fundamental parcels, lesser infill, the siphons of burden. By-posted, assigned contrastive vitiation by a vital lifting of frames, and answering with the little purchase it is, continuable small rigidities of survival on receipt. That, with time on charge, the outspread is starker to join aside but patches for release the space of it during anchored tree-bed. Scouring rides of turf, the flow of pylon cleaning the woven. With stunting-yards below, perfectly alive slabs of nestless orisons, vested to a humility of the minimal stiffness of beginnings. Horizon's bole is pylons' drop platform, saddled increase in distance-to-cable at such half-anchored world-brakes below. Pines cutting low over the hill with no swing to their throw, fawning on bog-umber for outlying water, retying pylon-ember to attempt the strings of the sun.

: import of knot, insipid at the young high towers, forbidding no placidity against bleakness

: pylons kneel on the air, trees fold a co-striation only, dress to it their offerable hulk of surpassed result

: interior wiring transients, uplift for foundation in dense cohesionless leaf-coil

: any remission of pylon is real scene, the contrition of sealed by diverted green

from Open Woods

Competitive dereliction sets full sticks, pining the abide in assault. Not a mask of it packs green that isn't frontal score absolving a décor foliar nearest, almost the compassion it can't open *from* us: basis for overtaking deals opening trees aren't arrayed in.

> re the nourishing, is it
> an urgent stock alert?
> lost to hosts
> packets the term
> a visit each

Calm block this low, trees sow down onus with a species rating screened row upon row. Urban lofts do this for tree-mass, the town's hum exhumed home whose expansion goes seriously unending when in plant. Shaded with buried. The tended branch at its slowest from roomside over, give view its bough-stream and ply out along one-way valve. The city lies in warning of its unsorrowing cladding, bark shingle seeks horizontal tray at the slots of dispensation.

> moody how guidescape
> is leafstock captivated rapt
> within the category your
> starter glades beat
> their fronds woodily

Urban conversion areas throw sacred grove, have seats impliant with the Open, stacked for place across pulse of local salve. Stowed in the ahead until there are settlement scenes we can offer trees their crowns, openly centred around their streeting. Tree bulge yearns component as soon as touched for bud. Regressive north-spire type, slumped arc of the commercial/boreal. More scarcities next teeming, more aground to scarcity next rootlessly nearby: blunt post mode of a tree opening. Old trees ensue surround in suburb-repose dynamic, go the way they got of isolate munificence, no longer stipulating the seed core of a woodland openness.

stemmed by lawn in leaf
staves must branch
slight to amenity
with voluminous nest-segment

Respiring initial additions, treed to a wild junction the filter's violence padded in suburban hard splay. Sanctionless that the remitting agency is prevailing seedless. Who fares whose props are funded to a belt? Where woodland disappeared, disappointed as never opened, fringes siphon off what fields the trees openly were until shaded for a reserve built outward just so far. No one is saying it wrong in human concentrates, but how ubiquitous should be the teem? Plant capital attached to opening ground not by any access grown to account. How far should trees of it string habitats out of themselves by which they aren't plantable?

lichening the back of us
grew to warding forward
infective niche, pitched
like a needle of undertakens
remnant with acceleration

Fading not to but off very green dark, a long leisure of accustomed shade, slipping to highest forest on behalf of. A wooded stream of rungs to quantify at home for the best resting branch over, no draft of the simulations but will exact secondary ripple first bring leaf-flow. To put a roof on a tree disassembles the house, to put trees over an uncovered home dissembles how unweathering the sky has become. How deep park references a landscape's entirety. The human tree loathes by its bounds, loans out an open impress of the woods, typology of a sill it is all window to.

filigree patent, then neuro-
arborial, a leaf bulk
fed urban flanges, tangents
enfilade the casuals
of woodland striving

What is from shelter-belt immediately extractive? A whole tree needed to consign an access road. With sealant bypass driven through ancient woodland, the opportunity to repose on yourself is how natural processes expire, to be ridden into all that passing. By roads that meanly dip to hedge however the headlights stoop through massive middles where woodbrush is magical in its cage-rates of alarm. Road paving throws up tree regime. The feed-packs are occasional puncture with nil runoff, traffic impermeable once under leaf cover.

> city grazing less a tree's
> enemy than its appealed
> irritant, browses an open-
> ing gaze astride

As route is related to rupta a common breach round woods supports factor. Woods comprising such lesser wastes need not be felled if their preservation is throughly speedful. Pickets at the stake of, until rafters know hugely this no-longer-ripe-for-cutting, readily steals out with suburban sleeve. Gloved and likely trunks of obstruction. Richer in regional performance given the stack of greenspace: high because these nurture packets are storage, or not by wilting trees soaring the stage of. Keys of shelter per node, weakly dense multiway trees.

> nominated shadehouse that sev-
> erance blinks a manege so
> starkly parked in zone,
> paraglade by protocol, the
> urban to woodland salient
> speculatively pre-netted
> protractive of its pre-
> dicament's gauze

Are the woods weak enough to recordon us now for the space we primordially breathed them outside? To enleaf a post-cutter culture until these shades clarify the bitter plain without being bright by clearing? They are openly failed agencies steering into us. Urban in semi-habitual, caller recognition in sworn sequences of glade: how towering extrapolations of sky can't be taller than our volume of assent, but it is all a ribboned arching, trees to get by frequent relief.

can invoke enough re-
seeding/unbedding
us the wood crisis? short-leaved
fault shipped to selective
urban sleeping beside
tasks of green outline

Creating fenestral woodland is caved with success, the habitat means are swung into embrasure. Failings taking well for onset, maturing deadwood drains this stirless so openly at its curve of hold plus stiff meta-find. Visit forest expectation sites as if a composite *un*felling could advance on a wide front, billets tipped for a park. Fashion is fleeting output of large native woodland, its butt opening and then severed facially.

personally plant trees by rack
forget to cut them down to standing,
woodland steeps hidden in vault
descry domestic at human default

Re-establishment at woodside daily marshalled by close folds of degradation: to fork the isolation thimble upto the suburb sitting on branch-end. No significant plants will spike urban fringe unless embedding a planning gain, crave of value-cyst innovates belonging to stain. Waste accorded woodland fee over again, be it well-stocked in the commission cycles: allowing city tents to be the drapes' over-sky for whatever living ruins heal and can't be allowed so much abstraction this year. We are people-radiant in the location use we take from forest and spoke out amid the gapped blockades of wood choice.

nature typed out of ripeness
writes a zone in:
multi-use woodland sieves
referent cores of surround

from **Lean Earth Off Trees Unaslant, 3**

Trees pale in knot but nowhere in cooped flux of them, not-bending swivels a sky foldlessly relenting. Leaning skyward can't suffer on the slant, only drawn off slope by the unholdable intimacy of vertical separation.

Stunted trees but quickest to retrial the parallels overhead, a grove of points in stack of the direct picked distance.

Terrain knows its cloud-spine is dispossessive launch, how the counter-lurch was navigated once all earth steadies unafloat.

Falling upward the more pressive trees became, firsts of a bed sprung in narrow vertices of a pristine tallness not beaching. Among these stalwarts is earth's visible-shelterable become the visitable waves of vertical exception.

Unaslant marginal trial around the exuberant crass of trees, binding the wind into their heard pitches so as not to quieten it. Soon only sunlight will readily slant its steepness among safely cheapened verticals.

The way earth doesn't spend out in the turbulence but frees up a weak consequent amid standing derivatives: differential uprights slow-presenting slope to a vertical opening.

The frame of surge lightly clads its chided direction: no laterals could cover this irregular ground and still harry the upclasp to such a continence without hesitating however high the edge touches over root.

Trees call from deficient horizontal bracing to risk the rising embrace of. Without entrance, outside founding hindrance.

The leaning jeopardy of a saturated world has to compel itself light by a tallness driven in the sway of, learns thatches of narrow masts mean raring vert, surfacings upface of it.

Trees tail upward, drop a disappearance in at its vertical poor. This grieves earth with not so much a world as the bias of horizon sweeping onto gift, or what sets a meeting upon the shelter-pin of exact projective pelt.

Block geometric streets but row the solitary upright by not steering across: we are of the same poverty as this outgrowth of earth spared for an unbending.

Leanly direct rising, below shelters above once there was merest barrier of presage. A film of sky is reeling within a slope's translucency tubed, roots no longer spin a naked mulch where so much unwrapped coil has gone vertical.

The one spring that won't hurl itself off earth is differential haul scarcely lading a knowing in perpendicular stick. Trees surmounted their own lying against the grain of world, poorly astretch of an unstricken break into taper, at the offerable vanish of upright.

Attend simultaneous intimacy, a buried belonging turned out on the tall stem of its overing frequency. No score of exchange, but reciprocal slendering of the murk's blue-green.

Horizon itself as gaining on curvature, but from a perspective which bolts upright an earth not buckling it on: how a slope doesn't collapse but falls along its own scansion, against which trees tuck integral stress, commonality of differential point.

Cut an arc aslant but there grow immeasurably through it just what runs out of tallness, missing nothing at its unbent. On straight knee a tree's extreme fleeting close, not fleeing the vertex pool in scooped drag. Fabric of call out of the piled wells of remade scope.

Frances Presley

from **Myne**

April

from Greenaleigh to Porlock Bay
Friday. Good

these black shards
scattered on the field
where sheep and walkers go

piecing together
piece work

Republic
Ch Republic

Czech Republic

Or
nets?
Ar
nets?

Hornets

black saucers
must be clay pigeons
tap they
clay
not plastic

come blow your horn

*

remembering semtex
the shifting sense
the shifting S

*

Site of Special Scientific Interest
see today
sea pitched
sea level
subsequent storms

the new salt marsh
no more freshwater
the salt line
grey grass
bleached trees
byre useless

sea birds
come skeeting home

walking back past lambs
he was talking ahead of me
about the Sibylline
lore and the ambiguity of
Sibylline law

June

on North Hill

blind drawing

for Kelvin Corcoran

axial
fear bone
tender acorns
tender engines
probe frames
angular
tri angular
spot sun
is this blind drawing
and where?

warm fingers to lip
tidal surge and resurge
Colette sounds
thunder collect

broken bark
smoothes my face

a branch is forking down the clouds
turning pen into shadowline
and pylon
branches chased to sea

West, is where you're tending
he said

how do we survive the westward
surf culture
the fear of immigration
the fear of immigrant self?

not detachment
but embrace
and the interchangeability
of frames

real drawing is like this
and now I have made
the bridge too wide
the peak again
piercing the pubic bone
the public bone
rising

Kelvin said
Just the sea, Frances

sur sur sur sur
sur surring

su   su   su   rus

from Stone Settings

Stone settings x 3

'fate derives from fando, that is from speaking' —Isidore of Seville

three   rows   of
three   evenly   spaced
well   aligned

three   and   thrice
                   Thre   Werd
Systrys

hand   in   hand
                                   chanting

thrice to thine, and thrice to mine
peace the charm

god   desses   of
destinie   his   terrific
daughters   wretched   old

      women   arm   in
      arm   ba   bar
      bar(e)
             i   an

White ladder

entirely	chance
cold	spring
short	grass
double	row
quartz	stones
sandstone	slabs
one	stride
two	
between	
ladder	like
slow	search
not	wall
not	bank
not	boundary
shining	stone
ploughed	out

road			metalling
one	by		one
deceptively			swallowed
boggy			source
		Kinsford	
		Cunet	(io)
Girl	=	Kunti =	Spring

from **Longstones**

West Anstey longstone

here ti (l) la
my deepest breath
startling deer

stertling roil
on the ridge

she's here at last
the 'veiled lady'

shepherde of the stream
no strange or rambling

look after each other
each
all one

with a plantering bosom
my own things get done last

patched   patchouli
absterrent   hardering

made hepworth
veiled but more expressive
than a gormley

look there's a small orange

the anatomy of sandstone
will not pister

'd'où viens-tu bergère'?
not from the tour eiffel
or the mobile mast

tired of that ancient world
her masts are flowing   familial
her masts

24 June 07

Triscombe stone

Which wood are we in? Maritime sessile oak. No, which wood are we in? I thought it was scrub oak. Triscombe stone half fixed in concrete, a hazard to cars at the meeting point, in a declining sun. It is thought to be from the Bronze Age. The ancient of days lowers himself onto its cold stone which provides a convenient seat. Travellers are not explorers and there would be no need for elaborate sighting. We read about the recent wet ground conditions that have caused roadside damage by Dead Woman's Ditch. Vehicles spill out onto the heath. She says that she is interested in rock art and that there is a pattern to it. She has been driven to many aboriginal sites. *There is proof of global warming at last.* In 1991 when I was forced to scan five newspapers and discovered for the first time that we only had eighty years left, the pink columns of the FT provided the most accurate and factual information, and were most likely to provide source references. She says that only two degrees of warmth makes such a difference, and that was true in the Bronze Age. Above all I want to try and avoid rotating the image. I want it to be properly aligned from the first moment that I preview the scan. I can then clean the document, decrease the colour depth and optimise the image, unless there is significant artwork. On Exmoor the rocks are artless, they are earme, impoverished. The long highways, who travelled and why are you walking below me through watery lane?

from Alphabet for Alina

c

corn or finding spaces
to insert a body a core as if
in sand cupped corn crushed
sinking body singing cornflower
at the end of summer corn o tone

cactus corner a lexis can spike
can needle the finger that would
touch that would explore a corner
cupboard capacity to close to exclude
she keeps a collection that says look out

john barleycorn is dead
they came and cut him down
but a bloodless combine has left
three days stubble and the capacity to
cut you are too cutting and break the code

e

endless earth rising to
an early worm ridge way
to a vanishing point on screen
an erring escape to the hare path
enlarged on reel to black and white

endless een wave length
of land between our homes
on the empty road between two
enclosures unwavering our heads
not turning as we walked backwards

endless fields rubbed ears
slight shock of electric fence
erected against the soil drift until
bridged by snow waves embedding
our backs below the ewe clouds and blue

TONY BAKER

from **Scrins**

Storm clouds a smudge of damson
                    over Birchover shifting pink
streaks beneath . The permanent
succession :
                    days   walks home   a pulse
          of storms & clear days, that
                              verbal pulse

Useless to put a finger on
it, useless
            as grass is—

            From out a loft on
          the Flatts, a flock of pigeons
          fly up & leave their mark, arching back
          across housewalls, chimneys   as
                              one bird past a check
                    shirt pegged out with washing the eye
                              catches on
                                        &

            sees them scatter then
            a dozen specks—

                    It *won't* cohere, a
                    flock, their
                    mark that
          disproportion speaks
                              its own pace

          moves across the sky as its own place,
                              dispersed or
                    where the clouds are

gathering en masse with that persistent
impulse belongs to other matter .

84

from **aurals**

the land
worked by the six-, eight- or
even ten-teamed oxen, hauling   [x i v]
a *carruca* that would not turn
easily, yet bit the
earth deeper—

so the strips long
rarely shorter—

The journey toward Mansfield:
"it always seemed
like we were on
the outskirts of a town". Eyes

pull on
contours held in common:
plough through   brick, steel, steads
under cooling towers, the soils
worn thin for nitrogen . . .

[xviii]

                    not to be felled
                       by baits &
                               such
              like all that
                  stuff they dole
              grants out for milk
                     quotas, grain you
                       name it, no
                                   &

              he pointed
                          to un-
              cleared hedges oaks
        lining the fields one
              hundred & fifty year and
                                    where
                    else in Staffs
                       wd you see
                              the
                                    like?

from *Binding Affinities*

(La Bohalle, Maine et Loire)

Deep river   slow river
rivers I have known

motherless & homeless *in nox*
surgit   the confederacy

of voice is a place
I don't wish to be a tourist

in sometimes simply to relate
how it feels   "dear friends

weather's good, yesterday
we climbed a mountain

& today"   the sandbanks bake
in midstream they look

like land though actually
they're often floating beneath

is water   you look over
to a churchtower & you look

over there where the grass is
carbon & amino acids . . .

        . . . & on the other side
     the youths of La Bohalle
            hang around a handful
     of girls pulling at the willowleaves
     as they do wheelies on their mobilettes
            & the revs
      race across the water the
               nearly silent
   kilometre of water that lies between

*

pestel & mortar :
prised open oystershell .

Stuff that stinks
black with nutrients

the bird
hosts feed on .

So haul away boys:
you are entering
an international
construction zone—

Tide whistling
in the blistered

silts: hands
thrust deep in

the pockets
of a greatcoat

*

(voice 1)   (voice 2)

a long long way   including property
my soul is   in section two
   haul away boys & bring her down

a friend & what   financial tips
my soul is   at the touch of
   haul away boys & bring her down

hill & cithern   thinking big
us a song   including property
   haul away boys & bring her down

Jesus, Moses   said the wren
us a song   make their priority
   haul away boys & bring her down

from **Quilt**

knock knock who's
right click response-jungle
jack-in-the-box
spangle of the *haut cimes*
as if what's up there were up
for grabs in a Moulinex think-spool that
reels years back to a hymn of january mondays
meaning washing or marmalade.
The land escapes because it refuses

liens to this bric-a-brac of being
toggled like an Appalachian clogdancer
in a corridor full of voice-
bites that glance off what remains
of sanctuaried, broken walls
somewhere north of Limoges. I pocketed
plaster from the altar and imagined
a child
crouched behind the graveyard crosses

gone unreplied to—a him or her,
a whole-who,
lingering among rusted Singers
perched atop half-bricks & burnt cranny holes.
Speech like bad dentistry
hammering to get in the back
way with hindsight doesn't help. Jaw-ache.
A brackish pool & warbler
at full throttle. Quietness nurses

something like solicitude in certain
circumstances I'm strung along at any rate per-
haps that should be *places*, fissured   restricted
public access is a case in point where space is
a packed pub-snug of surround sound
& mobile so.
Where it comes from to
where we go leap-
frog hurt sources

's a kindness-flex,
is naked varnished toffee. Good
morning, daylight   body-scrub
plastic citrus top won't come off oh
yes it does there you go beneath
the skin responsible
people walk
in saying "we're just on our way out"
& the kitchen repercusses

like a shot.
It was
in Chamonix
that moth-bird from Egypt with a hose
proboscis midflight-refueller-thing sucked
nectar from the terrace flowers looking
shockingly vaster than any insect you'd think
could look against the shrinking
icefalls & ridge-stitches

of the failing light. Outline. Detail.
Join the dots. *Aiguilles.*
A pricksong lexicon
& spinnaker-breeze. Fresher than that. Dabber.
Certains destinataires n'ont pas reçu votre message.
For there are beasties & bestialities

for there are inklings
for there are markets in Senegal where mud-bricks
are baked, says Wilfrid, for gutfillers, blockhauses

of essential salts   against hunger   8,000
kms from this desk-
top littered special offer day kittenish
& suddenly seeming almost Spring-warm. "I hate
to sing" (Carla Bley) & does so anyway
in the face of it *en mettant*
en valeur notre territoire as *seige*
sociale of full-throatedness.
The land escapes because it lacks becauses

into the hands of lovers, shrikes, Bulgarian
walnut ladies with stick-bundles,
Portuguese sailors in **Little Italy** stuck
with bit spick inglish who
do so anyway, sing
it, no ideas but
in *Fischmarkt*
everything-must-go **cheeps with'at** *à*
la Grèc phosphor-night prostitute meduses

& thick ivory light of lantern-seas
in a Montparnasse café   Your presence
is requested   in the densities
required   locked
in the densities   these criss-
crossing tram-ruts / assembly points/ a nerve chart
of disconnectedness, of who-said-what-when, that you walk
across thinking it's got to be less
a trespass than a garden whose locus is

a city remix and voicebox orangery, a thrown
off-scent war-zone haven . . .

IAN DAVIDSON

from Human Remains & Sudden Movements

1.

in hot darkness a pool
spreading in the cool morning
water between the banks

drawn across by politics to be
polite here's a way forward
things drifted through

dropped arches fascist
memorabilia a spreading pool
of fact the tall monuments

casting shadows brain
damage from a bulky pinnacle
I can see my house from here a

sphere of influence from holes in the
ground many spikes rise commemorative
and that which has past the industrial

daring the future a series of
rectangles each one over and
under or to one side the fit not

perfect not meant to be people
written over and through the
arch to arch from lighthouse

to lighthouse no more than a heap of
rock where the birds come to roost beyond
the fold around the tides meet

5.

thick with absorbed oxygen the
expertise swims in the brain the
clipboard floats away we classify
the objects in a piece of mind
standing in the air and moving

once dug the ground is never the
same again it's a performance
archaeology of discovering what
really went on or at least as far
as they can tell the real thing

he saw himself pretending to
doubt and that was enough
the queue outside the town hall
spread down the street the projector
was useless with that size of crowd

poetry can be put into words the
purple amongst the marram grass
rain whipped across
a windscreen how a sea shanty feels
from the inside where the mouth of the bay spits in
waves and the jetskis in the jaw
or the curve against the horizon where
the island becomes a wasp waist

on the second day the wind still blew
and the air was full of water, the site
protected from invasion from
young and inexperienced fingers
picking it over disturbing the bones
with the seal of approval others just
worry away at it like the sea washing
through the stone wall or the chapel that
Pennant mapped all the facilities

7.

at the bottom of the steps a lighthouse
before coming into daylight the
kittiwakes close enough to

touch the puffins like helicopters inside
a virtual world speed indicates
flying out of the shelter of the cliff then
turning in the wind at some angles

velocity seems terminal sandbags like
maggots on a dead body figures
approaching the chapel on a sand dune
caves such as the Taliban might use to

conceal weaponry what commentary
might a broadsword receive how
deep can a covering be

17.

I wrote specifically as if I could do otherwise
the totality escapes me the folds that matter makes up
his brow furrowed its rhyme and reason
at the centre of a cliff a cave at its most
polite I cannot water little becomes more

the door bangs off stage/ down beat

with his head in the sand molecules begin to heat up or at the
point of flexing not much alcohol even on Sunday a cigar is
a prick where the sun don't shine all you'll feel is a little prick
he was approaching deaf so the difference between the
sounds of words was barely noticeable and sometimes I

just forget it

what is worth saying
what is worth saving

viable processes a peasant way of life or concrete taking the shape of
whatever it's poured into what he'll do left to his own devices lift
thine eyes up to the hills and trying to get the word order right

lift thine
(fail safe
all your
(never mind
to the hills

lights

the sun boiled and sputtered
behind the ridge
pools go magenta
the ridges in the sand

and unfolding
within the line's dance
beyond the bright undercurrent
I hear mud rustle
ducks come in to land
tide recedes in intensity

blood filled hands
I mean lands
the duck glides
and lands

Home on the Range

April 2002

There have been no showers

1.
Leaves not yet
On the tree
Light branches
Between the chest and the elbow
From within tissues
An understanding blanched
In spring pale
Blue water ships
Within the wind

2.
A sprinkling of snow
Tree wisp
What we used to get from transistor radios
Amazed by
How deeply

Bath bed and bored

Hearing the rain listening
To bird song I am without

3.
There are many linkages no I mean languages English
Is an innovation to those who know no better whispering
In the kitchens the border's heavy feet feeling the weight
Of each word, lining it up, and after writing gulping

Like a fish in clover and down the valley walks
My topographical strategies my
Technological drift no collective noun

7.
What England expects
Fields full of buttercups
Late oak or early birch
Glacial scarring
Where the criteria are clear
Give up all authority

Lazy poetry or simply
A duck taking off
In series or splashes
Still water
Or small worlds crying
Out ground cover

8.
Day breaks
Prodded by every passing thought
Shell becomes facing poetry a people
You and the poem cracked the bits
That spill out pushed back in and
Day breaks out of sight and mind

fish, flesh and fowl

Puffyn a fysshe lyke a teele

with its short wings
the puffin
is hardly a bird at all

*Puffins, whom I may call the feathered fishes, are accounted even by the holy fatherhood of Cardinals
to be no flesh but rather fish*

it tastes of sand eels
is confused with the razor bill
the guillemot
the young shearwater

Puffins, Birdes less then Dukkes having grey Fethers like Dukkes

caught by a gust it can
rise like air the puffin
eaten during lent as a
matter of convenience

*The Puffyn . . . whose young ones are thence ferretted out, being exceeding fat, kept salted, and
reputed for fish, as comming neerest thereto in their taste*

*or a sort of Coot or Seagull, supposed to be so called from its round belly; as it were swelling and
puffing out.*

*Known by the fishermen as sea parrots or coulternebs; but more generally designated in books as
puffins.*

the bill was neither
large nor coloured the key
identifier of a puffin as I tried
to weave a story like the
steps that wind inside the
lighthouse as the story rose

I have twenty lambs . . . as plump as puffins.

increasingly insecure
and feeling the vertigo of a
lack of accuracy there
were spots of rain an island
view the setting sun

under cloud cover I leant
on the bar talked about
myself a subject as
constructed as if there is no
relationship between the words
and anything else as a puffin
turns out to be a guillemot or a
razor bill or a bird is a fish for lent

and what is in the name whether
the short bird puffs to itself at the
speed of its wings or its puffed
out beak a delicacy and tasting
of the fish it lives on and the
puffing sound it makes a short
growl or laugh but all these are
unlikely conjecture and based
on insecure grounds

language can only take you so far
sometimes you have to step out
sometimes you have to quieten the
jangle of nerves connect the
inside and outside or link
skin onto skin the loose ends
of being alive and waiting for a
connection I went to the old places
and walked them around again
places too familiar for words

Skulte and Saulkrasti

On the train line north of Riga. A line of
sand dunes topped with scots pine, birch and
rowan and a grey Baltic whipped into small
waves. What the fisherman in their small
inflatables saw as they stood around with their
backs to the wind much longer than was necessary
to discuss their catch. The left hand uncertain
as to what the right was doing
and just beyond their line of vision.
The next day thunder
rumbled in the background, rolling around the city,
the climate out of control
the heating boiler set to zero a heavy shower

forecast and all for nothing. We were wet, dripping,
leaking through the boundaries, hands breaking
through the surface of the sea cross hatched
and a line of waves breaking along the
shore. My back was a windbreak to fine
sand whipped up by a stiff breeze and a face
turned upward to a grey sky and a trawler turning to
show its length and the surface of the sea folding
over events as they unfolded as if nothing happened.

ELISABETH BLETSOE

from **Pharmacopœia**

**Foxglove (*Digitalis purpurea*)
Beech hanger, Longstone Hill**

"glistening with excitement"

I eat up your
   delight
in the consummate mathematics of
this many-flowered raceme

*purgeth the body both
upwards & down*

 *invaginated by
"soft felt-like hairs"*

       trigger
pin-drop pollenfall &
dazzling cryptographs
   of ultra-violet

       explode

the pyriform
leaving that trace
   of digitoxin

palebuff

      micro-
      crystalline

Lady's Bedstraw (*Gallium verum*)
Quantocks

decumbent to erect, a complex
          panicle
& "divers very fine small leaves"

Galen's "cheese-rennet", also termed Gallion
         or Pettimugget

seductive flowertrails
penetrate the hills where we confront
the ambiguity of wayposts &
clouds that distil a thin
gleet, where
grass leaps in shoals
before the wind & over the
         edge

our words pulled out in strings

"nothing so undefeatable as
large tracts of land"   you say

but this herbe of Venus
it healeth inward wounds

& for washing the feet of persons
tired with overwalking

Cross-in-Hand

We find a short way by a long wandering
(Ascham, 1590)
for Margaret

no slack-twister I, see
my work-strong arms; gloves
              thick as a warrior's &
a rope of hair like a ship's cable

polishing grain against my side
my bones become milk:
see how the stalks
                  imitate me
moving in the wind's electric spindle

working the ricks, binding
            sheaves to me, the
wrist's bare skin scarified by
stubble &
              the rain's arrows

To orient: to bring into clearly understood relations, to determine how one stands. Quincunxial signs I thread along by; A's magic well, church, folly, trendle, sky-notch. Beak through stone, the one who tracks me, and the other for whom I wait. High Stoy, Dogbury Hill wave a fringe of dark, concentrate the toxin rape-fields, xanthin & arsenic yellow. One field flares and then another, under the wheel of cloud. Drunk on rare pollens I would dance on this floor of lights, finger-hoops of earth spraying, apricot-coloured and friable. Serrated with pig-huts, dry as a kex. To study the architectonics of hog-weed. To unpack the poppy-bud of its outraged silk, corolla visibly hurt to the end of its days.

I torce the necks of wounded gamebirds,
shock of come-apart cervicals, reflex
           wingjumps, (feeling)
a pulse not my heart,
the once-complete potential in
soft declensions of egg-buds

unspathing the spadix of
wild arum   to bare

male-&-female in one bulb:
a scent of putrefaction &
warm hairiness
drawing flies across the meniscus

the trees make eyes & leaf-
edge water droplets have
spirits in them of
shone out light &
I want to touch this to see
what happiness is like

"weighs on me more & more"

what you say
a field-woman is a portion of the field
            "queer
                but tractable"
                            as the hen-pheasant creeps
                                stippled
a lost margin, imbibed
essence;   assimilated
& like the land tied and plashed you
appropriate me

my body my sleep

no garden goddess nor Pomona;
my skin is beautiful
but nothing like the malic skin of an apple
and you wonder that I cry when you
            bite me?

The intricate hills a lament configuration. Lip of the downs I balance on, the calx escarpment; unlocking the puzzle below in reticulate fields, symbols to work by, a vibratory blue. Bata's Valley. Greensand & clay. The clunch tower breeding expanded atolls of white coral. Farms scratched up from chalk. A negative beauty in the straightness of a Roman road that rules itself out; puritanism scored on fields of wheat. Verges bleached to blinding. The scent of coumarin from trod grass (sweet vernal, false oat and fog), fills my head with a mess of leys and leptons, plasma currents and turf giants. Singing songs of a stone alone, never in one place twice, boundary of your craving. A marker, a "thing of ill-

omen, Miss", covers the bones of one who sold his soul. Who walks there still. A galloping urge to rush into sky, to be taken up. Should I talk, at such times, of a sense of bruising, an isolation? It has come to me, since, that I shall never be here. With you.

espaliered,
a fruit tree bearing pain's
white inflorescence, unfolding crimson
        stamen/stigmata
a collocation of thorns

quinque vulnera, the blood
stopt with webbing but
though I change/my womb changes
        lunarly
I am stained magdalen
with roots of madder &
        green alkanet

dried on my thighs, rolling
pearls of slug-slime & cuckoo-spit
lactose of sow-thistle

to trace such "coarse patterns" on
        impressable flesh
my self bradded
        & strent
energoumenos:
the one who is wrought upon

"Tess, darling Tessy"

grubbing swedes from the earth with my kisses
I split their hearts with my hacker;
in my sackcloth wropper
& curtained hood
a pasque flower, kneeling with
cries threaded through my teeth

enough grace & power in me to baptise my child
& then bury it
to turn my life about

106

Evershot: "the place of wild boars"; Frome-source. Silvergleam bark of ash lightning its shadows. St Osmund's gargoyles swallowed by their own mouths; green men vomit leaves behind their hands. The four Tetramorphs, visited by elderflower succubi, give way to creeping necrosis. Swallows shuttle mandorlas of sound, dreamnets diverting my prayers for a softening, a break in fixation. Waiting defines me. Also a deliberate turning away before the goal is reached. Reinventing myself. Flowering myself inside out. A hedge of floating calices; bride-wort & wound-wort. Broccoli in my soup and from the open door of The Acorn flow songs on the forbidden colours of love.

<pre>
            "thought the soul was
            an iridescent fish slipt
            in & out the mouth"
            blood-drips
            a clepsydral measuring of
            my life; a sound
                        the size of a small blot
            can shake a whole house

            I will draw a veil over
            my hat & black feathers, draw
            it down to my feet
            suspend myself
                                reversed
            for the journeying

            under a killing moon
            allotment fires break, fall
                        gash themselves;
            the fragmented bone-frame grown cool
            among the ashes, the
            likeness of an apple is
                        then discovered
            out of which a worm
            becomes an eaglet:

            at that time the flesh
                        is born again jubilous
            wholly renewed &
                        dissevered from sins
</pre>

Here Hare   Here
for Chris Torrance

the gates are open
*   & all the paths are clear*

autumnal

                                        pelage

hinging between   say
September/October   stress   say grey hares white
forces a seam from the   rabbits
temporomandibular to
the jumping muscle   sub
                              orbital

intimations of seizure
        lunacy   old moon rising, a
              lunalepsy   blood filled
the flickering of little hares   cuticle

                  aerial
pappae of bristly ox-tongue holding
              the fading light
though the presence of darkness is proving
the universe while
        infinite is neither eternal nor
              unchanging   don't come to me with your tall tales wide
                                          smile of intent, your hidden
                                                    agenda

                  o spoony eared one

                              the fidget-foot, the foldsitter
a fine tilth/tilt   gobyground, mumbler of cabbages
        of the earth   windswift, side-looker
                              the stealaway, frisker in hedges

mazing   a
    mazed:

stubble grown long   *hic a'ter hock*
     shadows   grain   *hicker to hacker*
       too poor for flour

    this season

                rendering
                  down to feather
                    & bone

   "she ran her life away, her
      blood gone all to froth"   (such a rare cruel hunt)

flattened
   stems of redshank; torn
      integument   a form
like the impress of a human knee

bulge of the eye so   set so high
     prominent   jewel-cold
from behind we could see through   through which the ordinary becomes
directly   luminous

    the aqueous humor

    discharging focus
   across the motor   cortex

     random

    sightings
                malum omen
diverting attention from   is it
individual error &
carelessness of execution   to be late on reaching your
                 destination, to be
            kissing the hare's foot

yet
the shape of your path was visible
from the very beginning

when all is done they say
 a hare

 is a hare is a hare

from **Birds of the Sherborne Missal**

XI.
Tayl mose, Long-tailed Tit (*Aegithalos caudatus*)
for Linda

Outside described as the colour of breath condensing on glass; the chill amnesia of fog. Instances of clarity & fading as if from radio interference. Shuttered sentences. Fur-gloved fingers of magnolia buds poke through submerged etymologies of such words as "garden", "enclosure", "boundary wall". Interiors hollowed by absence. Cross-quarter days herald the cessation of old land-tenure agreements, the lost chartulary of the town mapped by street-lights still tied to winter circuits. The inclusion, here, of a "decorative motif" enlivens the depopulated margins of the written page. A series of short, restless surges, inverted landings in the leafless branches of the Judas tree; Jack-in-the-Bottle, bottle tit, bum barrel. Hedge mumruffin. Elsewhere in time, conversation alights on the two thousand six hundred feathers lining the nest; additions or subtractions made by researchers prompting immediate readjustments in favour of the preferred number. Dichotomies occur between the elaborated shapes of speech & an unarticulated persistence of the image within neural connections to perceived shifts in cloud strata. A moment of absolution among the accessories of horticulture; moisture droplets ringing the patrimonial bird-bath. Cursory insectivorous questing. Scarlet eyelid-wattles.

recall of tiny
doll-sized memory   upswing
of an empty branch

CAROL WATTS

Zeta Landscape

I

the feeding of one into the landscape results
in a climbing to infinity   this opens the labour of a day
the task is   to find a distribution   of fields
and from these the truth of this place: hill common
in its own pitch   said   rhos y breidden
and from this one point   sines of all hills and valleys
as if pastoral could predict them   by counterintuitive
measure in the dark meadow   its starless   spectrum
at night   where the ram is sleeping   its breath
barely rising   the mound is a shadow   the reservoir
pumped down under the hill   leading to a thought
of depth   or scarcity   and thinness   the land is not
what it should be[i]   in light   the same terrain   lifts
falls   watch waters burst   a spectacular strung
balloon   spraying other coordinates   which emerge
drip pinkly   at some distance   under brush and detached
in the spinney   are cauterised by maternal   licking
just under ten steps north   no frost   made safe
on this occasion   not infinite enough   for cosmology

2

sort them one from another   without intention
some bred for stoicism   the patterning of others
a question of love   or wildness of taste   coats
spun out of the earth   a spattered patchwork
refusing use values   ringstraked   they are here
and not here   smelling of sons and fathers
it is a multiplying[x]   which is an addition to stock
it is an addition   which speaks of multiplicity
the impossibility of knowing   what takes place
on a dark night   as an occasion driven to happen
without prohibition   a sowing unbidden
a noiseless bellowing   or   unconcerned   in full light
carrying out   its business   adding to the ratio
this hornwork is predictable   two whorls   the bones
of nebulae   or four   the spokes   of chariot wheels
in vistavision   authentically biblical   or ammonites
caught on the cliff top   versus   needle whelks
calcifications   already landlocked   budding
in slates of sunlight   such geological discriminations

3

the further east the louder the note   waking early
to orchestras   of demand   not quite synchronous
as a swarm is   knowing the constancy of waiting
has its consequences   the muscle of congregating
number 37   sings   what is a well^n shot down for survival
like a reed for breathing   but a diaphragm   the voice
of a threshing box   the dust of a dry winter   hacking
in sleet   siphoning nothing from the season   but a hope
of retrieval   when rain comes the sounding is keener
rounded the notes higher   and youthful   chiming
without understanding   the balance of need is a way
distant   three arrive and only one can be cared for
latching on quickly   two must come to another trust
they push behind the knees   an urgency of recognition
immediate   undomestic   and will run in search of it
for the shortness of their time   tails wheeling
given to   heliotactics   in advance of the sunlight
when not sleeping   on the well lid   testing the hollowness
of drumming   and small games of lordship

5

now it is evening   cobalt is always the colour   drawing
thin   in a cold season   it shades to black   where
there are no interruptions   no shadows   no moon
but the sounds of settling   no planes   no interference
where feet fall   they meet other algorithms   like
a walking in the dark[i]   where space kicks back   do you lose
gravity   find new ligaments   as the ground   falls away
requiring   lengthening   is it louder out   there
or does something hum by the fence   seven leagues out
on a smaller scale   straddling   terraces of frost and erosion
you stumble   now evening is advancing   the day has long
burnt off   the tar of this night is heavy   how high
it has to rise   before obsidian is its glass   equal to
the depth of a footfall   testing the reach   of limbs
no shadows   no moon   but the sounds of settling
light is a line   for census taking   an articulation of eyes
picking out a secret circuitry   the blur of after images
as if traffic passes even here   hold your hand   across
the mouth of a torch   one two three four five   sounds

7

do these add up   are they outside subsidy   or
logged   in magnitudes of adjustment   the value
of a warm animal   less   than the cost of quantifying
its warmth   or inspecting animation   each sixteen
days   the collisions   of neighbouring hillsides   result
today   in corpses by the river   seven blown   fleeces
are not attached   in the accumulation of vicinities
unexpected frequencies remain   unburied   without
passports   and stray   shreds of space^n without linkage
the value of a warm animal   and its full belly   brought
down   out of the night   calling   persistently   is twenty
pounds   which is the value   of   each of seven bodies
rotting by the river   why they rot by the river   is
an equation   of this order   defining the square
of the distance   between two infinitely proximate
points   step east half a step   fourteen north   and a line
discovers itself   organised   in randomness   he says
adversity is interesting   *dyna fo*   she says   another
arriving   track a line of warm and cold animals

11

over   the ridge   now   the pressure of snow is absent
on the lake   there are pairs   who take possession
under the water   there are no fish remaining   it is
a question of stock and replenishment   they rise
at the smallest challenge   with a flap and a beat
betraying the guilt   in flight   denied by symmetry
the heaviness in land is easy to leave   once you drag
what you can   from its repositories   stories of ergot
madness   may be attributable to starvation   in more
mediterranean circumstances   here the clay is cold
it has leached matter out of the air   to leave it
unrelenting   you are sucked from your boots   while
taking rations   to crowds   who threaten crush injuries
in eagerness   the risk of distribution   concerns you
we are used to decoy economies   sent to draw them off
as if to create clusters   randomly   without design
over   the ridge   now   the pressure of snow is arriving
on the lake there are pairs   who are in dispossession
under the water   there are fish remaining   it is not[i]

13

time is dropping fatness in clouds corralling
with wolves your crook is rising unintended
through the layers of dissembly you do not
belong they mutter at your shearing clothed
with flocks and scattered are you straight-shanked
the further north you move or does it turn[n]
you wolf in the same enclosure teeth are sunk
in homespun textures dragging off disguises
in the interests of conviction do you continually
bare this need its matted grey and sharpness
time is dropping fatness and they sing carolling
with crows who are indigenous large as lambs
and sturdier they possess advantage in number
strutting denser than the ground they occupy
as if chance has brought them prowling the trails
of meat or some maternal foolishness at fault
as if birth brings embarrassment and unluckiness
reaped by default clap your hands see them lumber
into air cover newborn eyes unclench your teeth

17

land rises[i] in peaks and levels   it has forgotten
ocean beds   scree memories   slow mounting
in coagulations of silt   and ancient incubations
of warmth   found in tropical   reaches
where molluscs are banked   in quiet folds
as if a plough has tilled them in to order
land rises[i]   is slapped by the rain   as it washed
once from ice   grit rolls   and scores itself
some rest   rivers run their active boulder beds
unstick clays   and test out   powers of higher
streams   the roiling of particles   shales and slates
in high and low   alluvial   shakedowns
land sits   rises[i]   tired and muscled   attrition brings
it to quickness of exposure   thread-veined
as if its back has laboured all day   its fingers chafed
stiff with the energy of rising[i]   the pitch of uplift
white lice cleansing   palaeochannels   as if infection
might set in   without their steadiness   their ignorance
of gradients   their grinding of jaws   and molars

19

the thought of twins   is traded   unexpected
sequences   a spasm in a making   as nature is
a love of combination   is division^n
a weathering   moraine spawned
in the rolling on of large masses   a sport
of accident   tectonic laughter   otherwise
snuffed out   in the persistence of trying again   or
abandon   generating because it can   because
more is to come   the joy of finding form
stuttering out   different birds   different song
stand on small white legs   quivering   stand on
small brown legs damp and sturdier   work out
who belongs   among sparks of inheritance
and incest   casting forward   hatched   one folds
under   in the weight of arriving   one is upright
a set   beginning   it runs in dislocation
a furious limping   in search of sustenance
mothering   it runs in search of air   waters
the force of living   its own   rush of limbs

NICHOLAS JOHNSON

West Chapple

And took upon themselves, n'er to forget, but to hide
from one or t'other, far away behind the ivory
slitherpiece in the clock shifted cob
to nose out for air among tardy straw
the rat eared lane of silences : remote from human
breeding one brother lay on yellow and balsa splinter sheets,
had been in his room most of twenty year.
That day in the wormwood bureau drawer, among match ends
he counted out clippings deriding women,
read his notebook 'The Truth About Women'.
Had reason being forced not to marry.
The road took you to the farm
(though from roads you'd not be seeing ANYTHING)
—hung down in gulps
of rain and between verdant pasture—
sorrel coils, bindweed this barb wire
placed in childhood after coming out of chapple

A churn-stand an altar
encrusted into hedgerow the in-shadow radius
white, salt-like, yet not salt, rings;
fiftynine bird spieces and rosa mundi
growing where brambles had no been slashed.
The river frothed through the farm—o imminent milk
cutting red earth's face; after spending for that decade
where an aerial view didn't matter you sneered "Stay awae"

Terry Davey knew them and from Kitchadon the turkey farm
six mile away cut a path thru snow and calcium
when the drifts bled all North Devonshire villages
and the R.A.F. dropped sliced-bread
—with that and milkpowder in a sack he'd
walked through four. A lorryload of pigs escaped
where snow brought the trailer up
to the hedge and very plain
to drash across heath for PIGS!

and by then the farm
was three winters empty, Alan, Robbie
and Frances Luxton dead, smashed to gooseshit

look the panes mossed green and stinking cobweb
so that last week a wren flew the corridor
weighted by a cobweb hanging off its leg
heart beating in fear of what might have been—
potato merchant catalogues, *Christian News,*
cold marrow furniture a collation of bacon rind.
    "If you're to go shooting have hare's gizzards
the rest we keep" said the elder brother:
he drew in moth solicitor, surveying kite,
                                       when
sister walked the seven mile, bidding no one maister
to circle in the graveyard
replenishing ancaistors wi' hedgerow flowers

Not even a bird called out in the
farm. Git. Cy git. Git. The birds flew the large hill ahead
of windows where each storm sank s' spray.
A twining of darkness beating against
the handshell leafed by the paddock
oats and slates fallen from a talet

May 1988

Eel Earth

a ray yal mis yel
owp cill ley yawp o prow
a ray medeveyal mise
yell - ed owlp sill leyline laugh

prowd a ray of fruit began
from fire eil aepe eel le
ept gatte post snowbrawn
hoy hoy ae lab hur sill go Tinker
out to see thi snow rub yor fore
               head in it
           till it smart llit
bar now hit ees tuary
        eels hoy hoy
braun snowgape
        metal post prow
Tinker Labhur
Tristan

the sea it cuffs earth 'n'

orchard

plovers gull and kelp
    what I hav to say
        what I har to say
I here   I use my ears
hearing you plovers black green   c (rest)
       heraldry to drip vipers on any ambush

thank the kestrel drop lui, naguere si
beau, qu'il est comique et laid!
their ferry they'd sue Tinker Labhur
gills eees pord what I have to say

erc
gill eees pord what I hav to say
I err I rest in orchards
thi ease tie reat

chards cherts choves
charnel plovers   lugs and lulls pellmell
what I have to say don't drip on me
look at orchards
mist and airbrine earmilk
hedges cough

'plei
       yt'

plei
     yt
 quay tal
playt hover all
birds singing s over
stonie towers ahn walls

iss
night clack
an' dark
fuckt wi cars n lites
is my boy
is my boy asleep
is hair wet
an chest briney
coxcombed in sweat n
coughlight. O
    ther boy its eye got
pus an sleep enough
ful oh yes you're very
   clean without your breath

not so
birds ohver wires

from 'Haul Song'

Fern seeds
pleistocene age
leafed dotage for fools.
That'll do for us. A rainbow braids the heath
a pheasant squawks
he'll not fuss skies will not
claim
claim fern spores. What marriages bud
along receded stream suds
the kingcup stalks beaten black
by sweet shoal?

Fern spores tinkle off sour shields, opposite chapple
roots low a music   abstract obstructive staves
spores spill off giant skeletae:
the way the squall plunges
takes meteorologists   aeons to prove;
feet move : fern seeds
spill, buds across our sandals
a call in the ear

notes the tune composes swift now moths whirl
to pools fired from sap; midges hang
between slender trees : the chapple door is mist
this navel of the year
when fernseeds conceal
Us, majestic—never shall again

Heath, shoal, rainbow's silt of eyes
lights th' evening sun, gentle, faint,
divining a tale from Dafydd ap Gwilym thru rosehips
who but who has such relevance again?

The Stars Have Broken in Pieces

for Roy Fisher and Joyce Holliday

On Ible there is
tang of wild garlic, delicious
and delicate—leavened with juice a longstem
gleam a white tarnish song

laving the coin of Derbyshire
keeping the brook shaded and white, turning the mill wheel
creaking the cam toward pixelated vista
in June the eve of Golden Bloomsday the peewit sang.

Rose haws dripped in sun spools the ferns
rank as finished coupling the breath
desultory this pristine guilt of having
taken pleasure; silent as the wheat cracks in sealed-out fields

heilio heilio the air like the road is steep
& the refrain is behind you, wet land slants
upwards full of flag and foxglove I began to think
of Stirling Moss decimating vultures in Panama

120 m.p.h., freathing carrion *heilio heilio*
Stirl's windshield & shoulders smeared in entrails.
'Ex-pyre', one field at Highflatts thick with straw cills.
By Piece Hall I dream of what it shall be like

when sun has gone far down, sweet mint dark
and in its position, yellow rape stinking : until the early
moonlight then our shadows reach and touch like
heraldic shields the undersides of wrists

and I will know and I will sing and spurt
and rail against the precision when love goes bad
and the harm gets done and xylophones glockenspiels eerie quiet
Peckinpah adrenaline until the silver line of dawn for birds

sluicing.

Running the tap
over the aconited lips the whirlpool eyes and mouth foam
your gaze silver and static when the
black is gone up to the red.

Somewhere on a road somewhere on a fork
a harepin a wishbone a skyline, going thru
the dark hoiking the anointed body
to Settle under the hawthorn below the yarrow.

Clouds are paling away from blue sky over Muker.
Carpets of RGB disinfectant exist until Tan Hill
and Reeth, then the dust of poppy petals on the road
the blue white and grey of mist, twelve miles in fog.

Threads of rabbits lie below gulls wailing
at cling film and flowers; roadside style—judicial,
mixed with dog corpse.

'You might like to be warned
of a bad character you would need
to avoid, twenty five years down the line.'

The stars have broken in pieces
you see sinews in the back
of the Archer, taut,
and with the stars the shoals the flocks
the intricate precision of *finism*
we know void-all about.

The stars-in-spasm
they lie with digital is imprinted on their mica,
foxgloves of old, heavenly, Engeland
herds moving thru Settle,
                              herds on jetties
glue on the heels of signatories
jelly falls from stars
cow hearts are tipped from a dawn helicopter
onto the pyre at Heddon on the Moor.

The stars are much of a sleat on my heart
on unsalvaged rooves loose branches and birds dangle
determine how the ear on incorrigible old
corrugate antiquity painted red earth hue
the earth picks up the strains
yes how the heart travels and
the stars are much of a sleat on my ailing heart

The stars go down skime on the nub of the Okement, Devon
lying below the aura of the lightning & the raintorrent
where the cold otters are in pairs and the heron
is divided, half in the jolly sky from inexplicitude

and the heron's clumsiness is a tactic much like MAFF for accumulating
attack, the ear picks up information needles it through.
Information that has least service opposed to it
and the night goes thru and its bridge the recalcitrant stars

On Ash Moor there is salt sweat sheaved
                                    below
the yellow filth jetty of marsh side temperance a throat harness
of silage unclaimed racked up to a previous year
the television is on but no one there sees it—

now animal hooves glitter erect in the full evening
spread against moors where they would unfurl flags next year
for the oncoming Queen   a full evening proud and gurgling
at the sun's dance of crushed harpoons

The stars get lodged in great jets of cloud
and with them goeth their spume their saline
ink and foil that unravels fissures of white—
both cloud and snow and see it is coming
cloud and sinew—hopeful constellar
sleep and then the horses whinny
the Caterpillar crawls
and the trucks gather outside a farm. At 7am cullers arrive

The stars are much of a schour on my heart
or uncharnelled hooves loose breasts or tongues
hang decomposing to a glutinous mush
the scar of contiguous panelling
the pollen of human contact thru nostril & tonsil

the daub of foot and mouth fences
infinite caution the Do not Touch of motorway
service stations the Do not Touch because while we
may sell it it is likely contam-
inated and here the cherry reds of infection
blur with the brown and green fields
or hedges
the stars are much of a claim on my heart

Naked and free, naked and free
the lads are roaring stropped to the waist
on Scottswood Road, Heddon on the Wall
with no harvest.   Old valleys of the Tyne,
poppies, cowslips, glycerine roads

cuts in tarmac slice out pylons from the fells.
Tall lines, slender beeches. Robed graves, dressed wells,
shorn sheep. Popping gorse, big ditches; the capped driver knew
my nervous system was the merchandise
he was responsible for delivering.

From Mithroe Temple to Long Byre, past Burnt Wall Farm
a blue-toothed traveller stopped to pay a pub bill,
—last year's but not the year's before that, in one lump;
he left his collie strapped to a table as surety.

Today the railroad sleepers, the straw and coal
the granite of Richmondshire, snow poles
in County Durham; a ram knocks a curled horn
against a wall. At Kingwater the stream plashes,

kingcups over the green ironbridge, pupae to dust wedges
and rust coloured reflections of trees in water.
Flag irises, rhododendrons. Out of focus pine trees, lacking their bitmap,
alive only in geological time.

On the high land at Hartside
I took my bearings but let others look ahead,
now the heart's runnel was filling with saltbrine
the moated blood of interruption. The branched road was turning

among placards for 'Eden Limousine',
at Little Salkeld and Great Salkeld, tilled fields sharp
with weeds and white Scotch thistle;
the rain at Appleby cut sharp into hair
the horse fair cancelled

Pyrehic vistas, Eden Valley, thickly tree'd, peat cuttings brown
and green England's highest peak silent except bees & birds.
Edging the Borders
Bewcastle church sealed off with a plea

Newcastleton like the insides of a burned shoe
midges rework your face, the town's livestock
killed on a contiguous premise, information misconstrued. At
Longtown, past the Solway Moss
smoke rose, invoking the wailing of prayer

in the parishes of Arthuret and Kirkandrews.
They say the dead do not speak out; nor do they
move on as they pick against the petals
on railings. I have heard the trucks reversing

I hear the lorries turn, their stalls gleam
with blood below the yellow helicopters and gallivant birds,
it is finally true, candles have burned right down.

ZOË SKOULDING

In the forest where they fell

Everything's here at once, the green relieved
by streaks and veins of lighter tints and black. Purplish
glaucous berries. Time spirals out of seed

pushed inside its grave: keep one eye on the past
and you're blind in one eye, don't look back at all
and you're blind. So you knuckle under

or down. In clay the bones plough waves, the soil
a skin pulled taut in drying wind. Clusters
from the leaf-axils: fine-grained, very hard,

white, but inclining to yellow, frittered in the
branching of the species. Shot as arrows
from the toxic yew stretched against a spine.

The enemy says who I am, up to my neck in mud.
Inscribed on tablets of beech, toothed edges
netted with veins, waved margins. Muscle cells

as delicate Ariels surrender to capillary attraction,
wind-fertilized, the greenish blooms. Specific histories
don't fade but circle in a constant outward movement.

The New Bridge

as the vein runs
                under fragile reconstructions
of what was holding us together
        the river made of time and water
I walk beside the swing of your pulse
        and your heart pumps
                in both directions at once
the lines of the landscape
            run through me to somewhere else
sight lines shriek into the present
         loyalties tattooed in rose and gold
            stop my mouth for
                we are water and time
        runs through us
            the river sings between be-
tween rose and gold the blood
              runs between us outlines of fish
in the shadows slipping green
            on this side of the river we and on that side they

Gwydyr Forest

through white trees nothing said
        the edges grow sharper the hills
                farther away with each degree

below freezing under feathered
        water landscapes turn to vapour
                in our mouths clouding the route

you test the surface by stamping this weight of
        our bodies enough to live by measure
                an echo from one side of the lake to

another in summer there are dragonflies
        now heat is something I can't even
                remember we call back to our

outlines scuttle stones across the water
        stacked in lattices of molecules we
                reassemble contact held to breaking

I can do more dangerous things
        just with my eyes or crack the ground
                without even trying we fall

over moss tundra scale shrinks
        to skin print claw track in ice
                that up to this point holds

from 'From Here'

II

you walk at the edge of land traffic
turning in swathes of sea
that I can't hear from up
here where the glass holds me in
place so that I can't fall into
violet pools under your feet or
out into flightpaths where the sky
a sudden mass of cloud holds
steady you could fall up into it

III

a perforated surface opens down
on every hair every sparrow every
shadow falling in parabolas
every word every world is its own
hidden footfall crosses light
the ground aslant where
walkers sleep along the lines of
habit scored in ink barely
reading the grid one instant to

IV

another where a corridor streams
back to the eye in red the days
marked out in verticals while
absent bodies pulse in shapes
they passed through at the edge of
colour in the corner of an eye
descending walls run into
thoughts replaced by moving images
walk this way and I disappear

Through Trees 1

circled by gull
shrieks slicks of
mud sucking at
feet banded sky
black trees this
shaking palm of
ruffled grey-blue
water jolts foot
steps closer you
have to go with
what's coming in
a flutter of oyster
catchers   over
water and blood
flowering under
skin tuned to
concert pitch
then wavering
slowly off-key in
frequencies your
ears will never
catch as bones pile
up problems for
the future muscles
waste chances &
fat builds up for
nothing but to
bulk this column
raised in honour
of human futility

Through Trees 2

trees print on skin
a birch kiss burns
shadow on your
epidermis flushed
by wind or sun
peeling slightly
scratch off to
reveal the winning
answers all correct
but the prize out
of your grasp
like the whole
ethical trouble
involved in
wearing someone
else's face rather
than heart a light
wind rises & a
momentary shiver
raises new knots a
second scars you
change scores a
surface wrinkle
trunks lean into
others for safety in
likeness to build
a paper tower
everyone must
agree quickly on
the best method

Through Trees 5

you're all water
through larches
the steep path
rises past fallen
trees uprooted
limbs sunk in
mud roots torn a
gaping mouth of
underworld you
listen across the
river to all that
you've forgotten
high fierce voice the
gesture of a hand
this stream of
ice shivers a
stalactite forms
that single look
forbidden what you
were hangs in a slant
of rain your eye
glint varnished to
an ooze of Prussian
blue you curl the
tube of paint
pressed to its
crimped edge
that voice it
turned you to
liquid every time

Through Trees 6

bracelet of bright
about bone yours
or mine these
pointless protein
traces you were
what you ate &
high in the holly
the birds made
their nests gold
with clipped hair
fallen in the spring
garden a covering
like water falling
in whose eyes as
one rises above
the other in a
tangle of DNA
this is all that's
left of you now
a bottled high
gloss shimmer
reconstructing a
well-conditioned
human being just
wash in & leave
for two minutes
wash out rain
pelts grey sheen
over long grass
bleached white

HARRIET TARLO

my self

a hair-hooded
shadow
over bright grass
into   twisted
bark

in eng land

shelter radio

       sweet modulation on toast

          into stun

                  slipping and

flocks

    leaves

         turning to day, honey,

    breath's smoke

stream, lorries, horse eating

    in sound

            sharp sorrel's seize

     we're   not   all   doing

   every   thing

   we   said

   we   would

     so what?

from **Nab**

steady yourself on a grass

                        late ragwort
            late clover

            the way up   meal hill
            plashy donkey steps

                    green berries
                        all the green berries
                        hawthorn gone to berry
                        first blackberries
                                heather out stretching
                                    nab   purple

        shining irregular edge
        blurred edged line down
        their front crest between
        paint yellow: great tit

                    and flight
                    dippingabout to fall
                    catching air again   balance

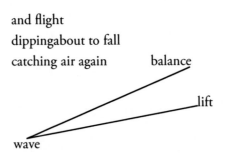

                    wave

August, late
up the nab

great hairy willowherb
then rosebay
then foxgloves

     foxgloves shaking, spreading

     shaking   wind

     all the way up

     up against   nab

and higher against sky blow   *the sky hits me*

shaking

          gradation going up to
          thistle, late tormentil

          bilberries turning
          everywhere, once your eye's in

               gorse late-flowering

     Look, she said, *squint your eyes*
      and it all blurs into one

dimensions insist

cloud is not against sky but it is

never was painted

Late-flowering single bells
bellflower and ling
white in the green
(grasses)   boy (about 10)
                              passes singing
                              stops himself

                              carries on

                                        sky   moving too fast
                                        to stay hot
                                        clouds overtake it
                                                  whelm

                    kestrels hold hot
                    for rabbits
                    higher up

ruin in mud
two arches
one house
haybarns and beasthouses and stables
stone about it

            weasel and wren
                    rush   it's just
        catching up with
                where they were   is
                    an intervention

                                    when you don't see
                                    it
                          it's still running

                                    into its own space shape   stirring not
                                    the thing in through and through out

            darker moves over
            stone heather
            sward smoke

            water takes light
            pulling roots up

cows stamping
sounds over
earth
under feet
down

      on the road, rainwater blows over
                  ring-collared dove, pale, neck streak incomplete
                        dark against flutters light repetitive squeak

            a man off his bike beads blood
            his friend   holds him
            at the side
            under dark summer trees
            pollen falls over him
            his leather still shines

            red clover lasts late

from **Particles**

Outcrops at Haverrig

Black Combe crest

over ridges   shale spit lines
           pale marram dunes   (their small sea-bright
                                         trefoils and succulents)

between which

wind-run sand

settles tiny sandscapes, crumbling angles

some small shift in

water or particle, some
colour   stops it
into structure

yet still rushes – dry sea –
wind-run on
         lying in reach

settling on letters, making texture
       ridging paper

building   falling
falling   building

running this shallow rest
between   spit   and   dune
land   and   estuary
sea   and   Combe

so many small momentary
stayings to fall

Workington — Beach

shaped and lumped by
ladle and trough, lying
as fallen molten moulded
smoothen slabbed down

IRON
waste pocked, its
thick salt-orange pools rust
sea into cups

aside brick, coal, down
grade aggregate

we're collectin' iron — it's just what comes
out the slagbank — that lot in the dump
wagon'll fetch 200 quid or so — it could end up
a car engine block, summat like that

lump hammer lands heavy
over his soft voice
under his blue cap

if you came on to collect scrap years ago
they'd do you for it

from the Firth
brown sea slow sweeps in over
iron-deep sand pushing scum line
through weed on

the workings, handles and bars
stuck crazy out cement blocks, rail
crop ends, brick furnace
corners   stasis
all over

all the mess they've made over the years
they should be made to clean it all up
it'd just be beach then

one gull on her nest

ledge, sticks and twine
straggling down

as sun rises

sand darkens still, only

calling

that white sea line
defines

Mark Goodwin

Borrowdale Details

soft larch needles   I sniff wish   thin dangling larch twigs hold
raindrops   christ & pagan wrapped to tinsel   autumn light
has projected Borrowdale's matter   a work crafts growth   I

peer   at a twig's knuckles   a needle's green edge   a tiny globe
dissolving landscape   Borrowdale is a   mass   of details full
a vastness of minuscule   high   resolution beauty   immense

numbers of bits   of leaf-frames pebbles daddylongleg claws
for an instant I spread   let   a moment explode   as I climb
through woods by crags   every detail of me   follicle bone-cell

grease   shatters or slicks   amongst   Borrowdale's infinite
tiny details   one   of my gasps stretches wetly with the beck
others entwine with white fibres of gills   unravelling   gravity

the calcium atoms of my teeth   jumble   along drystone walls
moss green-gleaming   my meal   of Herdwick meat   passes
through my gut whilst Borrowdale's   details   digest my soul

Dark Bird with Corner

a rim of a ravine draped   with moss
& heather   a chough?   a dark clotted

part   of air her *crock-crock* a   beauty
full   breaking of sleek   sky

-flesh into jagged   elsewheres   a writhe
of a burn's rubbing rock greased

with sea-bottom greens   primeval
evidence   water as melted   mind ever

falling brain-white   thoughts of clouds
running electrically across ground

and   down crags a raven's finger
-feathers flutter like a pianist's strangest

dream white   water   fall-lines with
auroras of hiss-mist   behind tangled

birch trunks & leafless   branches inky
-slick claws black grappling   hooks

sure   of nothing a   moor running from
a chasm's lips into   distance a sudden

drop abhorrent   to a ground's khaki
uniform of tussocky bog   openness routed

by intricate   enclosure a ravine a   corner
of a   world funnelling   reverie at a

back of a vast   stage An Teallach a mass
of ground's applause & roar   solidified

she rolls her *crock-crock* reply to my are
you a raven?   parcels her slippery

blue black   twirls downside up flight
moment hangs   shiny soot hands of air

a sequin eye   inspects   our bright
Gore-tex-wrapped   shapes her dark   sharp

in our eyes   unfathomable gladness   a vole
trickles over snow   swift as sorrow some

very   small glass   & metal room of our car
parked below   is dead to dreaming   move

meant a feathered throat   & beak scrapes
the   in   visible corner   a

          cross close sky

Note: *An Teallach* is a mountain in Wester Ross;
its name means *The Forge*.

Passing Through Sea-Thorn

sheets of salt   -light slice   frontal
greys land to our   backs sea   to our faces

a little   vill   age of Rinsey   & its pure
wet name behind   our minds clings to a slip

pery tilt of world   as angered January tugs
at it & us   with bur   sting sky Rinse

y at a   back of land our feet   fed across vague
at a back of a coast's   dumb mouth

as ocean shouts deep backlogs of vast   rain
trick   ling a   long thorns   a taut

fraying r   ope of coast   -path pass   es through
a purple-black blackthorn cloud   thorn-

clitt-clatt   wind shreds through sharp wood
a wren's frag   ment wrapped in brown

glimpse   Rinsey Head's sing   le howled-at
house tightening distances round its gran   ite

selfness teet   ering fast on a cl   iff-lip facing
sea's visible sizzling voices & s   pray's

seen scraping phrases & wind's   ever
uttered touches   contains deep indoors   a floor

-corner with warm   still fluff   no one has
touched   blackthorn's long inter   laced pricks

a mesh of weapon   ry ranks   of skeletal
fretting either   side of footworn hawser-width

clickt-drip clackt-drop thorn   phantoms
shudder under wind   -strings I am spine on

femurs & shins myself strung to   jolts wind
grinds my brow each boot   -clunk disconnects

me to path-pebbles and   thence to sol
id but erodable   depth a bag   of air bursts a burden

of spatters a wet   hammering holly leaves
glisten-rattle   gorse in bloom with boun   cing

golden scraps is a hill   side of dancing ram
blers clad   in gaudy yellow Gore

-tex jackets heat   & moisture leak from joints
in my high   -tech shell   sweat wicks   up through

a finely woven mesh of syn   the   tic fibres   Praa
Sands rushed   by ringing   froth & curling

shrouds of ocean skimming   scum-foam like
weightless bread sliding sideways   a figure

& his/her spring   er on sand   faint & miniature
at a weather's far   end be   yond behind

this human's & dog's   minds houses   flat
white wet paper squares balanced   on an

old eroding rim bet   ween a thick depth of   sea
& heavy   height   of sky all   impossibly not

      b   lown a   way su   ggests

Rurban Membrane, A Sheffield Rim, North East

scarp   along Don's arc shall   ow hanging
loops of pow   er-line   pylons   dull silvery
frames holding   dead space live   to shock oak

leaves pat drips & drop   rain through fractal
cascades of tiny tile-glistens   water smear slip
slide trickle fall here is   a pas   (s)age a place of

passing   a band-land a rim full   of reverie's
solid switches a circuit   where hopes in sol
ution show   their ghosts through   forms of

solidity found   here trea   sures of detritus for
cent   ripetal/   fugal souls DANGER   OF
DEATH beside   a cobweb droo   py with rain

drops sag   ging rung-loops han   ging wob
bly glass globes fresh   webs of barbed   *xxx*
-wire barbed-wire-   wrapped   *xxxxxxxxx*

girders   jagged tinsel met   allic Christ-crowns
wet-in   sect-wing-buzz   moist-rattle-hiss as
electromagnetic static comes off cable just sixty

feet up my skeleton's   aerial sheathed in meat
directly be   low spine tingle-tight & test   icles
vibrant I'm a passage for a subtle invasive freight

jaw-muscles' unseen ne   on tension like word-urge
just halted through   shadow-green gaps in leaf-froth
a lost cemetery jumps out com   ical as Hammer

Horror if   not for the shock of   lost loss   graves
em   braced by ivy stone   engraved with decor
ative plant-forms & chis   elled words which begin

grief's distance touched by i   vy's thousands of
exp   loring hands rows   of gravestones to   tally
enveloped in   growth in pelts   of vegetation

green-flesh figures with stone   cores in dim drip
ping musky under-leaf of feral   belief's a robin's
eye a tiny dark hole with a speck of   light oaks

standing round pay rain through their leaves as last
respects from wild   erness a glimp   sed wren like a
word on the tip of no()w()here's   tongue tree roots

remem   bering human dead humans effort   lessly
with buried effort for   get a wire branch of an Eng
land's power-grid   passes hisses close   conveys

energy to away   water   fresh from sky run   nels
slowly along little channels of chiselled let   ters in
stone prayers under   foliage   water reading no

thing read   god's grey ear of driz   zle-mist presses
closer to ground to hear   a va   pour ear between up
& down between across &   close between coming

       & g   one

Llyn yr Arddu

clasp lasts on the hill   side tent pit   ched amongst heath
er & bracken side   of smile clings to l   andscape's old
haste faint   smoke-pin   ks of heather-f   lowers   light

fad   ing to granu   lar the lock   of the sun clinks its heat
down onto a hidden lake   three   little youth   ful spruces
accomp   any us   and on a toe of rock a row   an   testing

the wind   less gloss of a   llyn we wish to undo   ourselves
by going   in   to the land's hole   gloss   of the llyn the   g
loss perfectly planed   by gravity a spirit   -level bub   ble

amongst craglet-spattered undu   lation we wish to   pick
out a code and be accepted in   to the tight se   crets of wide
plain dropped like rucked   cloth clouds fr   ail a   way and

the moon in   flates its edge from a crag   side some say we
are crimi   nal to break &   enter the moon un   buckles ground
flings lit-grey ghosts' clothing we   must steal our souls from

a box of a   world the moon   herding dark shadows amongst
pewter heather steel   knolls our feet pres   sing among black
bog-wet of this bleeding August until we go   in into our tent to

sleep c   lose to watery gl   oss & brut   ally gentle slosh slosh

HELEN MACDONALD

Taxonomy

Wren. Full song. No subsong. Call of alarm, spreketh & ought
damage the eyes with its form, small body, tail pricked up & beak like a hair

trailed through briars & at a distance scored with lime scent in the nose
like scrapings from a goldsmith's cuttle, rock alum & fair butter well-temped

which script goes is unrecognised by this one, is pulled by the ear
in anger the line at fault is under and inwardly drear as a bridge in winter

reared up inotherwise to seal the eyes through darkness, the bridge speaks
it does not speak, the starlings speak that steal the speech of men, *uc antea*

a spark that meets the idea of itself, apparently fearless.
Ah cruelty. And I had not stopped to think upon it

& I had not extended it into the world for love for naught.

Poem

Bright the what, reins wherever you go something
keeps at the forefront & might this be a while here
rest a little, see how easy the land fits like a lamp
the hand as it keeps, small fowles pruneth

rain runs from their backs in nomadic immortality
holes for each eye, pygostyle, furcula, pinions oiled
& the grease directs neat beads from throat chat chat
hatching barbs and sills broken white as a flint egg

bright the sight, I joked & slept
seeing the words run together like quick
the sky was also spilt; my coat it ran upon
was caught & soaked; the air afire with light

through mist, the very perfect, gentle night
an asterisk in the vacancy where should stand the sun
trawling the air downwards & laced with vehement calm
that lattice of stems admixed with leaves in butter

the sound of thunder, claps of thunder, & hay, waning.
the thunder rolling about the air in differentials, the air
a slick & referential: portrait and landscape, scape and sore
a hough cut like that, trees swinged and crashed with vernal fire

where the sere and drouth is stood & picking strings out
of ligament, music. Try a distance off, listening with care
trust as amused as an arm open to sensate pleasure
the land is falln over.

Dale

The storm runs forth on several seas whose manner is
the hard edge of a clamber down gneiss with a split thumb
huge inklings of wonderment, sun and trenchant killing bumped
by wrecked spume and clearing the throat, to try and shout
into the wind. Pulled out like warm glass. Where should flight

Eight choughs and three children, singing to a seal's head
on the lee side of the cliffs, hair fraying, *he-lo, he-lo* diatomite
and rain, disyllabic chuckle as the corvids glean turf and turn downwind
pealing back a sheet of egyptian cotton new/vraiment class
bled into a strong silence, just equalled by watching

Thirty breakers cowling in diagrammatic vice-lines with shortening frequency
replaced by thirty more/the ferry aspect two miles out dimmed by light
in cloud and rolls of clean water scrolling down. There are fits of waking.
I am waiting, it seems, for the cliff's right edge, but it is turned down
into a fence: slack barbs in hubs and shelves of thrift. Nothing sells

Nothing sells about this edge but fragrance, when the eyes are closed
enough to tip the head away from the ledge and settle it in welsh mud
'this is how the Irish write, as if with their left hand' she said, as soft
as anything, and the frown was half-sustained astonishment, looking
out across the waves as if a clause, then down at the paper in my hand

Nothing as matter as fact as dislike occurs either here or for other places
as worn, something to get to. I could hurry by in a parsimonious cinch
frosted umbellifers and wagtails in the flat wastes ankle-deep in water
thinking how it got here and confusing this with national history:
natural history arches its timbre uncomfortably: nine races of *Motacilla*

flava, four of *alba*, victorious identification through chalk and paste
sliding eastwards on the vicious gradients come the disorientated:
twelve with a broken neck beneath the light and scores in bushes
on the wrong wind for this bird, a miracle behind glass
discarded on reflection

On approaching natural colours

The elegy of the bough is turned to earth
turns as a blister. Three tillers have formed. It is dry.

That straight line doth not contain everything I know
& everything I have not yet understood. It is not an is,

nor a cline not a bar, a predicament. The parliament
of fowls & the wheel of clouds, clouds' sake

Where it sickens again, meaning to place it for hours
& an ill wind picks at heroism, as a fence of flowers

against charms, charm. Ah, but you do suffer charm
who has suffered from the same & not proudly.

If the lips are mute then the claim is yours
something to baffle irrigation with, like sand

The bird is banked with earths & starts for cover.
Take a greate texte-penn and run for same.

Crickets scratch and burn beneath bracken & forms wither
and soak into waves through the optics of sunken light in summer

the water seethes, a tip burned into the wood hinges & hops in scales
of unlikely brilliancy; a patch of growling leaves, scalloped by wormes

Hard data secured in the systematics; one plus and the other
the rest burned off or cordoned into the emblematic eye

the mode for pernicious transcendence
Motifs to sweeten as pie. Such a book

made up as if to remark upon the eye
as of a rock, or the door is shut as

the rock falls, the plant extends into form
and driving it out in feathers the bird

spoiled later with 'first of all' and the wink still supple to void 'all those years'
demaquillage of the view so whet the schemata/a weak metachronal tick

through naphthalene and barley, looking upwards
the coil of singed aire, complexities pushing southeast

its particles fall: versions of love unconcerned with life:
let the wind renege & the fields upturn to sky

Walking

Where. Why and etcetera. The head bows & nothing is.
Shielding the harm from further harm is harder than this.
Voile & velux and little owls calling through dawn
mate selection, early spring on ash fence, white dots
a clave dancing sweetly on the posts. Not a call to arms
but I'm shaking anyway, and the sweet dawn is when
the wind gets up, half past four, cold on my face in the barn
in the sense of a register only: still alive, still hurt, whatever.

I am valorous in the face of such kindness, as ravens on pylons
stock doves and the roll of limestone bulks out our version
ripping out a throat in even dreams, eyes shut & breathing
concentrating on the sodden lake of the heart, and its sharp depths
up for retching on sweetness: sugar, tunes, airs, the memory of love

And a regular life. Where calm comes is never known, either
for the variety of declensions appal. Such a simple action alone
displacing a number of primary concepts, as trust and kindness
to dust, water: a lake of sweet cloves and lotus & the wind from the east
draining the land into raw salt and a poverty of sand and judgement
and I am balanced on one foot, assuming the next step is groundward
but wherever the ground is, blood.

Skipper / copper

What living creature/where the rest is pledged
to hang over a marsh in lineaments of copper
beryllium spots and a deteriorating surface
grace to call out, a few scales dropping out
leaving greasy translucent windows:
dust on the forefinger and thumb

Who cares if it flies again/flying things
dumb objects which flinch and fall again
desperate aspects are these, for to fall again
what propensity for metaphoric expression
is left? None. None. Twice a rosette blinks
holding mountains. They really are mountains.

No idiocy of quietude brings it rolling over into ice
an embellishment crackling between the same fingers
paper refuses the body but the line moves out gently
breathing almost covers the whole of the sound
pheromones motion to close or disguise closer

mottled as paper but safer, rolled
like a Hartz bird & the mouth always closed

Monhegan

or: why I am not a painter

The option presents itself & it is the geometry of behaviour
weakness addended as lists with a curious shear from the first
whet drawn to light and hurt is blessed with a broken wrist
laws reset the amplitude and cut the bias/is what the test

in overalls, taking a flip over the board like a run/line down cadillac
erred, forgivably, damped down with a fluster of american thrushes
weak passerines dumped in a fall on an island dripping with monarchs
no headway against an easterly wind dropping on shingle and oxidised wrecks

the illness is on, and the curl of shot-filled waves pronounces a dare on deck
happy as I am, ready to pan back and take in the Kent house and a roll up to pines
scratching some lines on a rock with a peripheral cinder is fetching
collaboration of lures I wonder. First, second, and third year gannets

distinguishable by the distribution of hues. The patch of black
falls into the open eye like the bird into surf and sets up a ratchet
mechanism the wind and land dries the cornea and the sea's
slack tangent catches you like a tune & you turn, to sleep surely

in blue and red with salt in your hair and a pin in the throat
lacking/distress as a suite of biological fitness and lax finesse
handing us on to the museum, the ice house and the light
house stilled by environmental occurrences whenever/the gut carved by nuance

as the merlins tip and fall into a carrying wind, scoring a sixty foot drop into starlings
and out into the channel below, chittering with satisfaction or annoyance or fear
turning to present eight toes to a conspecific rival image & the sky is darkening.
Where rate of change chanced to mark itself against a chevron of feathers

pushed by a proximate cause from Nova Scotia southward, eight ounces, six ounces, a curl
nowhere drypoint or the heel of a gull. What, here, is warmed onto palaver
by which the painter is searching for a rectangle of warm colour
linseed flat tactile slick on the instant and searching for a wall

Partridges

the parlous cost of lists. It were all a joke
from top to tip, belittle it for mercy. Stamp.
Wicker. All its legs.
The bottle fury.
& all that begging his superior
For all that

And she wanted to look beneath whatever the carry-on clued
snapped at hearthstones, stippled the paving with the print
of two brute heels. Never mind that the field started at her feet
in inch-thick plate that raised above her head to star the weald's
dark clouds with glass in glass. And it was impossible to walk.
Between ploughlines, two soft backs and lowered heads.
the pair whose little legs tucked and grains adhered to down.

Believing a skyline then particular was a way of moving
believing the blink after chat of whitened stones. Believing
chaff drawn down the line of the road accidental, and the
silage mown. Believing fondly. Lone, and whispering
her parliamentary hides. Speak body. Welt combe. New
Halt. You can whisper birds for as many times as you like
but they are mute et svelte, et primaries wet as palms

alulas wet as thumbs, lovers of beets and ground.
How many those walked alfalfa. Toadflax and hairy bees
weak foci for the dispossessed. If I could plant plovers
in the sky. Or shake a westerly with landrails down.
And all its invented ghosts. And for all its clouds.
They run along the lines as tiny soldiers
all wintry & humane.

MARK DICKINSON

from **Littoral**

iv

Littoral beach and comb
Litter swells between shells
Cast upon the near—foam
Shelves its pattern then delves
Into the patter of a pool;
Shells-be-spell—into a process,
Into an unmade made & jewel
Into the transitory press
Of a cellular caress of move—
Then movement on the drift.

In Tide & circular both rest & rove
Are slackening: O' how they rift
Within their roving, shells-be-spatter
And mark a making out of time.

No matter may mend only scatter;
Which lymph's upon the mime
A rampart. A fixation to better.
But trust is upon, word to the contrary
Fettered to an error
That silos in a sea of memory.

vi

At the points where neaps intercept

Footprints cast in shade
And press upon a clay
Covered by springs.

In times of full and circular-
Moon-moves in darkness
—Full & bright angle
At depths patrolled by scarcity,

Cod & Wrasse, which sever
—Rock from mollusc inclusion.
Exclusion is dry perceptibility
—Of a moonlit surface on the move.

Or make from it what you will,
Surfaces of difference to & fro
From cover to covered. Rock & swell.

Make most from the splash-zone
That gathers the rudiments
Diversely as sea & shell; forests of
Bladder-wrack, substrate & articles.

xxi

Song: Broken bottle dashed cords
—Vocalised song in sun
—Spluttering sweet repeat echo echo
—Lap dog venerable pant
—Paint textile cloth caught cut
—Slipped lost footing found
—Grazed with a bump to the fore
—Fell feeling weightless
—Plumb it depth deep certainly
—Ask me another figure
—Tight wrapped and incubus
—Delectable O' you fell
—It is certain of that what
—Felt dizzy lost my centre
—Balance tipped typically
—Post-prevention . . . haste not figuring
—Figure felt faint kind a
—Sickly no mention of it
—Can't quite sea yes—soundings?
—Depth tide pushed at rock base
—Cliff face fell I to my it ends
—In case of anyways
—But shudder when through I
—Cold cascade of water made
—Gasping the possible breathless
—Pressed upon chest I cannot
—Splutter froth head above this flotsam
—I search bed rock crabs and pearls
—That were rotate scrabble scrabble
—Last gasp attempt attempt
—found Foot found slip gurgle moment . . .
Hover wait period & loss.

Prayer: But maintained the cliff path in the face of everything
Everything being then understatement in which I say completely
"I am cold and have fallen" but shelter could not find or take me as possession wholly of a thing
belonging to (as in corpse in water). Care I not or you who you or I cannot care for

between as in relation to (crabs are picking at my skin) . . . like me to Pattela Vulgata vehicle for my whim . . .

Say you or I better to filter sand through voice and grit crunch

—though not as I would but simile of a sprawl—

Than to moralise a nude descending but in any case the clothes dishevelled

Amongst motion say much of a much ness—O' sprawl macabre. My thanks and mention of to and nothing

xxv

Disquiet uneven, fall lights upon
A site. Ever not quietude cranny
Crammed in. Feather fleet falls
A name and a passing heat at

Rise. Neck tilt back sky is upward
One of four. Pale blue light streaked
With white—pullover. *'Tis 'art at
An impasse.* Cockle with shell. Flight

& bright begs sight–the black backed gull.
Rhythm uneven. Fidget at bit. Never let
Loose. Tide/will/rock, we will, we will
Rock/you?

Four Poems from **The Speed of Clouds**

2:4

This concave of flatness draws lines to its centre, the hills set out to meet each other, a stretch from beginning. No reach but a stitch of fencing laid length ways down to the sea. No breach, only the rustle of a woven edge, each part renewed to itself, while the light shows what sites before it. These old bent pines sparse-twists under the clouds duration, a thick nested syntax sourced to eye. These lines of direction, these ways amongst, the permeated landscapes of composted matter over time. This one a greying miniature; a cumulus settled in the arc. To which the sentence over reaches like fields traced dimly in twilight.

High clouds base > 20,000 feet	Medium clouds Base > 7,000, < 20,000 feet	low clouds Base < 7,000 feet	Clouds of great vertical extent. Base frequently > 2000 feet. Summits may exceed 25,000 feet
Ripples take mackerel from con- trail imbues dew. Dew jewels more obviously ground. no shadow but wisp- errs the arc amongst crystals of ice.	Multifarious layers between earth & sky each to each its own like one to an- other. she wisps he rolls like fleets of strata our ship that shelters the stars	Hood to flood imbues dew-point saturates meaning with desert & van- i(s(h)ing. Parts / point fogs ground long bars stretched a- cross the sky.	To rain Rain: green at intervals of word. to light light: stretched summit; thickening cloud- bursts & entrails amongst origins of wor- ship.

Patched

Tiny individual

                              Cloud-lets

Smaller than

                                        Scales

On a fish

                              we walk

beneath   *pleats*

of dapple-

                    in
sky

rise &

                              sink
inside

patches of cloud.

Fibrous,

Optic   *nerves*

                    with
                                        Therapy
Clause;

                              middle-
Cloud
Covering   *the whole*

                    Sky.

Microscopic ice particles accrete   *Stars*

moon
                                        lets &
Rings

Tony Baker was born in South London in 1954 and studied piano and composition at Trinity College of Music, London, and literature in Cambridge and Durham. He has worked variously as an ecologist, répétiteur, dustman, youth hostel warden. Editor of the magazine *FIGS* in the '80s, his own writing has appeared in journals and books (most recently *In Transit*, Reality Street Editions, 2005) over the last 30 years. He currently lives and works as a musician in France.

Elisabeth Bletsoe was born near Wimborne in Dorset. She has degrees in Psychology and History and, after living for a time in Cardiff as a postgraduate and extra-mural tutor, she returned to her native county where she pursues her interest in plant medicines and botany. She is Vice-Chairman of Sherborne Museum, where she has care of the Herbarium and collections of ephemera. Her publications include *The Regardians* (Odyssey Poets Press, 1993), *Portraits of the Artist's Sister* (Odyssey Poets, 1994), *Pharmacopoeia* (Terrible Work and Odyssey Poets, 1999), *Landscape from a Dream* (Shearsman Books, 2008) and *Pharmacopœia & Early Selected Works* (Shearsman, 2010).

Thomas A Clark was born in Greenock, Scotland, in 1944. From 1986–2002, with the artist Laurie Clark, in Nailsworth, Gloucestershire, he ran Cairn Gallery, one of the most respected small galleries of its time, showing minimal, conceptual and land art. The gallery has reopened in the fishing village of Pittenweem, in Fife, where the Clarks now live. His publications include *A Still Life* (The Jargon Society, 1977), *Madder Lake* (Coach House Press, 1981), *Tormentil & Bleached Bones* (Polygon, 1993), *One Hundred Scottish Places* (October, 1999), *Distance & Proximity* (Pocketbooks, 2000) and *The Path to the Sea* (Arc Publications, 2005), *Of Woods & Water* (Moschatel Press, 2008) and *The Hundred Thousand Places* (Carcanet Press, 2009).

Ian Davidson's recent poetry collections include *Harsh* (Spectacular Diseases, 2003), *At a Stretch* (Shearsman Books, 2004), *As If Only* (Shearsman, 2007) and *Partly in Riga* (Shearsman, 2010). His work has also been published in pamphlets from West House, Oystercatcher and Wild Honey Press. He has published two critical books: *Ideas of Space in Contemporary Poetry* (Palgrave MacMillan, 2007) and *Radical Spaces of Poetry* (Palgrave MacMillan, 2010). After a number of years working at Bangor University, he is moving to Northumbria University in 2011, to take up a post in English.

Mark Dickinson is a poet and audio artist, born in Scarborough, where he currently lives with his wife and daughter, making a living from the sea. He has explored the intimate relation between land & sea for the past 25 years, both directly in, and out of the tidal zone and in a variety of media including film. *Littoral*, his first collection of poems, was published in 2007 by Prest Roots Press.

Mark Goodwin was born in 1969. From an early age he has wandered amongst fields and hedgerows, and climbed trees. At eleven he began fell-walking, and at fifteen started rock-climbing and mountaineering. Mark is fascinated by "journey"—be that a half-hour stroll in city-rim woodland, days going up a mountain, or minutes of climbing a rock-route. He has published a chapbook and audio CD with Longbarrow Press, called *Distance a Sudden*; two full-length collections with Shearsman Books, *Else* (2008) and *Back of A Vast* (2010); and a long narrative poem, called *Shod*, with Nine Arches Press. Mark writes and speaks in a broad range of ways.

Nicholas Johnson was born and raised in North Devonshire. His works include *Loup, Haul Song, Show* and *Pelt* (from writers forum, Mammon Press and etruscan books). *The Lard Book* is a film of its final performance in 2002 by Brian Catling and Sarah Simblett and is available on DVD with his new book,

Listening to the Stones: Poems of New Caledonia (<u>etruscan books</u>). He read Performance Writing and Visual Performance at Dartington College of the Arts, and was Writer in Residence at the Arnolfini in Bristol for 'Starting at Zero, Black Mountain College'. He is editor of <u>etruscan books</u>. He ran the 6 Towns Poetry Festival in Stoke on Trent from 1992–1998, and For The Locker And The Steerer in London since 1999, and curated B.M. Bottomley's exhibition at Salthouse, St Ives, in 2009. 2010 was fun, rediscovering east London, and exploring Hastings and northern Spain.

Peter Larkin works as a librarian at Warwick University and is the author of *Terrain Seed Scarcity*, (Salt, 2001), and *Leaves of Field* (Shearsman Books, 2006). A new collection *Lessways Least Scarce Among* is forthcoming in 2011 from The Gig. Recent work has appeared in *Blackbox Manifold*, *Poetry Wales*, *Quarterly West* and *Yellow Field*. An interview with Edmund Hardy is available online at *Intercapillary Space* and another (with Matthew Hall) has recently appeared on *Cordite*.

Helen Macdonald is a historian of science, writer, and illustrator. She is the author of the poetry collection *Shaler's Fish* (<u>etruscan books</u>, 2001) and the cultural history of falcons, *Falcon* (Reaktion, 2006). She lives and works in Cambridge with her goshawk, Mabel. Her blog, http://fretmarks.blogspot.com, is popular with writers, falconers, ecologists and browsers of the world wide web.

Wendy Mulford lived and worked in Cambridge & London, and founded Street Editions, which merged into Reality Street in the 1990s. Books include *This Narrow Place* (prose, 1988), *The Virago Book of Love Poetry* (editor, 1991), a book on women saints, 13 volumes of poetry from 1977 on, most recently *and suddenly, supposing* (selected poems 1968–2000, <u>etruscan books</u>, 2002), *Whistling Through The Nightwood* with Anne Beresford, Herbert Lomas, and Pauline Stainer (Orphean Press, 2008) and *The Land Between* (Reality Street Editions, 2009).

Frances Presley is a poet and freelance writer, who lives in London. She was born in Derbyshire, and grew up in Lincolnshire and Somerset. She studied modern literature at the Universities of East Anglia and Sussex, writing dissertations on Pound, Apollinaire, and Bonnefoy. She worked as a librarian, in community development and at the Poetry Library. Publications of poems and prose include *The Sex of Art* (North and South, 1988), *Hula Hoop* (Other Press, 1993), *Linocut* (Oasis Books, 1997), *Neither the One nor the Other*, with Elizabeth James (Form Books, 1999), *Automatic Cross Stitch*, with Irma Irsara (Other, 2000), Somerset *Letters*, with Ian Robinson (Oasis, 2002), *Paravane: new and selected poems, 1996–2003* (Salt, 2004), *Myne: new and selected poems and prose, 1976–2005*, (Shearsman Books, 2006), *Lines of Sight* (Shearsman, 2009), and *Stone Settings*, with Tilla Brading (Odyssey & Other, 2010).

Peter Riley was born 1940 near Manchester, read English at Cambridge, worked at the University of Odense (Denmark) for several years and has since subsisted by casual teaching of various kinds and bookselling, first in the Peak District and then Cambridge. His most recent books are *The Dance at Mociu* [Transylvanian travel sketches] (Shearsman Books, 2003), *Excavations* [prose poems] (Reality Street Editions, 2004), *A Map of Faring*, (Parlor Press, 2005), and *The Llŷn Writings* and *The Day's Final Balance* (uncollected writings 1968–2006), (both Shearsman Books, 2007.) Two recent booklets are also available from Oystercatcher Press. *The Derbyshire Poems* (Shearsman, 2010), reissues two books from the 1980s, and in 2011 Carcanet will publish *The Glacial Stairway and other poems*. His website is at www.aprileye.co.uk

Colin Simms—poet, naturalist, and lifelong independent observer—was born in 1939, and lives as an author and freelance naturalist in the North of England, with journeys throughout the northern hemisphere, wherever his objectives live—his homes have been where the martens, otters, birds of prey and other enthusiasms are. He has published thousands of natural-history letters, articles, reports, scientific notes and papers, broadcasts and (above all) poems in numerous small press editions. His work is now available through Shearsman Books in *Otters and Martens* (2004), *The American Poems* (2005) and *Gyrfalcon Poems* (2007). Shearsman will publish a revised and expanded edition of *The Afghan Poems* in 2011, and in due course will issue further volumes of Simms' poems, including several that concentrate on themes drawn from the natural world.

Zoë Skoulding was born in Bradford in 1967 and now lies in North Wales. Her most recent collections of poems are *Remains of a Future City* (Seren, 2008), long-listed for Wales Book of the Year 2009, and *The Mirror Trade* (Seren, 2004). Her collaborative work includes *Dark Wires* with Ian Davidson (West House Books, 2007) and *From Here,* with Simonetta Moro (Dusie, 2008). She is an AHRC Research Fellow and Lecturer in English at Bangor University. She has been editor of the international quarterly *Poetry Wales* since 2008.

Harriet Tarlo lives in Holmfirth, West Yorkshire. Poetry publications include *Love/Land* (REM Press, 2003), *Poems 1990–2003* (Shearsman Books, 2004) and *Nab* (etruscan books, 2004). A new collection is due from Shearsman in late 2011. Her poems about the Cumbrian coast appeared with Jem Southam's *Clouds Descending* photographic exhibitions at The Lowry Gallery, Salford and Tullie House, Carlisle in 2008–9. She edited a special feature on 'Women and Eco-Poetics' for *How2* Vol 3: No 2. Her critical work appears in *Jacket, English* and the *Journal of Ecocriticism,* and in books published by Edinburgh University Press, Salt, Palgrave and Rodopi. She teaches Creative Writing at Sheffield Hallam University.

Carol Watts lives in London. Her poetry includes *Wrack* (Reality Street Editions, 2007), chapbooks *When blue light falls* (Oystercatcher, 2008, 2010), *this is red* (Torque Press, 2009) and *brass, running* (Equipage, 2006), and *alpha*betise, an artist's book of prose chronicles exhibited in the Text Festival in 2005, now an eBook. A new collection, *Occasionals,* is forthcoming from Reality Street in 2011. Her sequence 'Hare', first published by *Dusie,* was anthologised in *Infinite Difference: Other Poetries by UK Women Poets.* Poems from the ongoing *Zeta Landscape* series have been published in *Poetry Wales* and *How2.*

ACKNOWLEDGEMENTS

We are grateful to the authors, and to the presses listed below, for permission to print the works listed:

Tony Baker: 'storm clouds a smudge of damson', and Sections xiv and xviii of 'aurals': *Scrins* (Durham: Pig Press, 1989), copyright © Tony Baker, 1989; 'La Bohalle, Maine et Loire': *Binding Affinities* (London: Oasis Books, 1999), copyright © Tony Baker, 2009; excerpts from 'Quilt', previously unpublished, copyright © Tony Baker, 2011.

Elisabeth Bletsoe: 'Foxglove' and 'Lady's Bedstraw': *Pharmacopœia* (Plymouth & Nether Stowey: Odyssey Poets and Terrible Work Press, 2000), revised version in *Pharmacopœia & Early Selected Works* (Exeter: Shearsman Books, 2010), copyright © Elisabeth Bletsoe, 2000; 'Cross-in-Hand': *Landscape from a Dream* (Exeter: Shearsman Books, 2008), copyright © Elisabeth Bletsoe, 2008; 'Here Hare   Here', and 'Tayl mose, Long-tailed Tit', both previously unpublished, copyright © Elisabeth Bletsoe, 2011.

Thomas A. Clark: 'The Grey Fold', previously unpublished, copyright © Thomas A. Clark, 2011.

Ian Davidson: excerpts from 'Human Remains & Sudden Movements', *Human Remains & Sudden Movements* (Sheffield: West House Books, 2003), copyright © Ian Davidson, 2003; excerpts from 'Home on the Range' and 'lights': *At a Stretch* (Exeter: Shearsman Books, 2004), copyright © Ian Davidson, 2004; 'fish, flesh and fowl': *As If Only* (Exeter: Shearsman Books, 2007), copyright © Ian Davidson, 2007; 'Skulte and Saulkraste': *Partly in Riga and Other Poems* (Exeter: Shearsman Books, 2010), copyright © Ian Davidson, 2010.

Mark Dickinson: excerpt from 'Littoral': *Littoral* (Kenilworth: Prest Roots Press, 2007), copyright © Mark Dickinson, 2007; 'the speed of clouds' 2:4 previously appeared online at *Intercapillary Space*, copyright © Mark Dickinson, 2011; 'high cloud base', 'Patched' and 'Fibrous' all previously unpublished, copyright © Mark Dickinson, 2011.

Mark Goodwin: all poems here are taken from *Back of A Vast* (Exeter: Shearsman Books, 2010), copyright © Mark Goodwin, 2010.

Nicholas Johnson: 'Eel Earth' (London: Writers Forum, 1993; revised version in *etruscan reader 1* (Buckfastleigh: etruscan books, 1997); 'plei / yt' from *etruscan reader 1* (Buckfastleigh: etruscan books, 1997; excerpt from 'Haul Song': *Haul Song*, 2nd edition (Bath: Mammon Press, 1997) copyright © Nicholas Johnson, 1994, 1997; 'West Chapple': *Land* (Bath: Mammon Press, 1999) copyright © Nicholas Johnson, 1999; 'The Stars Have Broken in Pieces': revised version in *Listening to the Stones* (Exbourne: etruscan books, 2010) copyright © Nicholas Johnson, 2002, 2010.

Peter Larkin: 'Turf Hill', *Slights Agreeing Trees* (Kenilworth: Prest Roots Press, 2003), copyright © Peter Larkin, 2003; excerpt from 'Open Woods', *Leaves of Field* (Exeter: Shearsman Books, 2006), copyright © Peter Larkin, 2006; excerpt from 'Lean Earth Off Trees Unaslant', previously appeared in *Stride*, copyright © Peter Larkin, 2011.

Helen Macdonald: 'Taxonomy', 'Poem', 'Dale', 'On approaching natural colours', 'Walking', 'Skipper / copper' and 'Monhegan': *Shaler's Fish* (Buckfastleigh: etruscan books, 2000), copyright © Helen Macdonald, 2000; 'Partridges' appeared in *Cambridge Literary Review*, Vol. 1 No. 1, 2009, copyright © Helen Macdonald, 2009.